Waiting to Fail

Waiting to ~~Succeed~~ FAIL

ANTONIO SMITH

Copyright © 2012 by Antonio Smith

All rights reserved. No part of this publication may be reproduced, distributed, or transmitted in any form or by any means, including photocopying, recording, or other electronic or mechanical methods, without the prior written permission of the publisher, except in the case of brief quotations embodied in critical reviews and certain other noncommercial uses permitted by copyright law. For permission requests, write to the publisher at the address below.

Driven Publishing
605 N. High St. #181
Columbus, Ohio 43215

Ordering Information:
Quantity sales. Special discounts are available on quantity purchases by corporations, associations, and others. For details, contact the publisher at the address above.

Cover Design by Trae Wilborn
Cover Photo by Rose DeVore
Edited by Victoria Kovacs
Interior Design by Brad Pauquette

ISBN 978-0-9858425-0-5 (pbk.)

First Edition
Printed in the United States of America
1 3 5 7 9 10 8 6 4 2

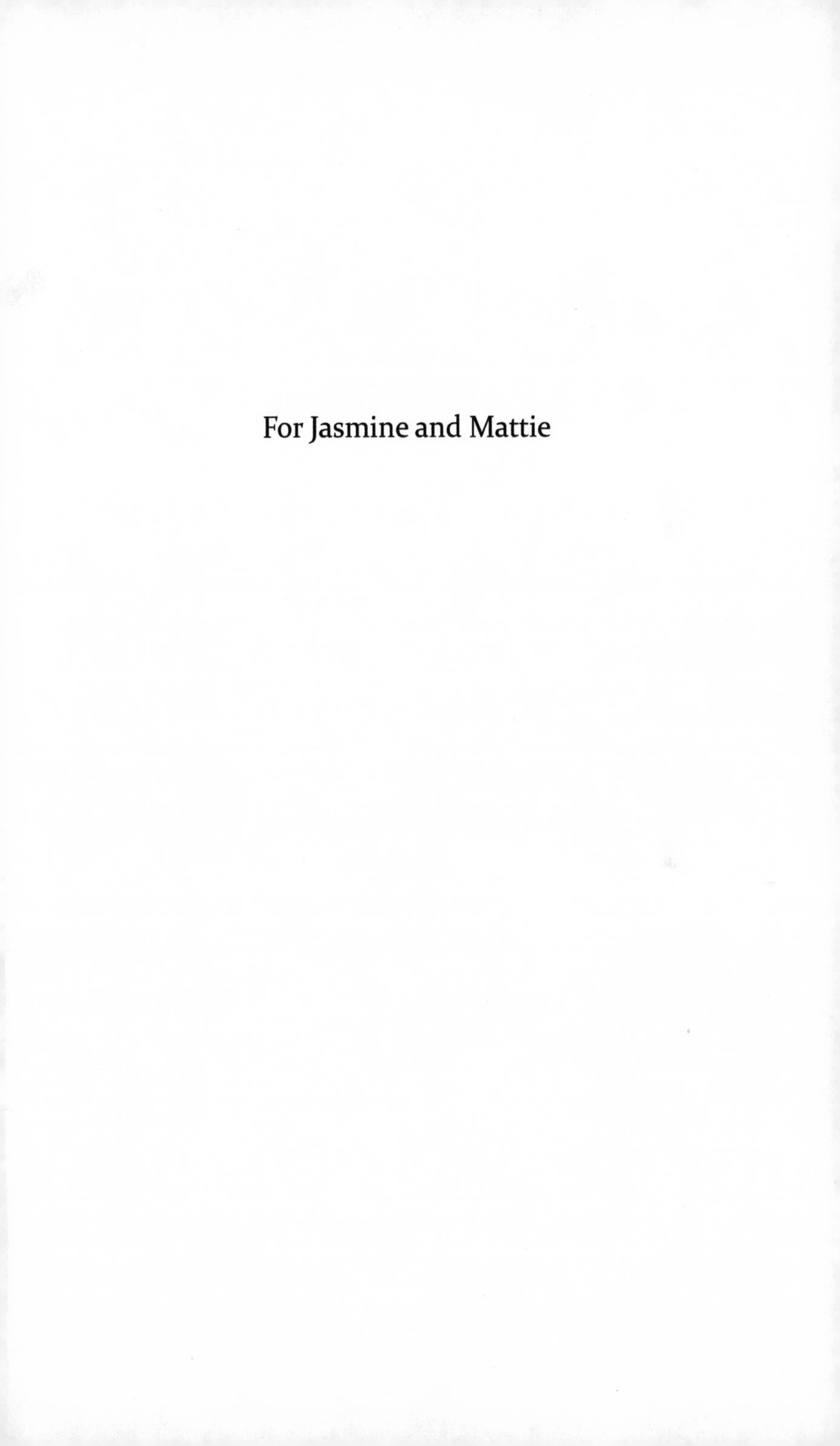

For Jasmine and Mattie

CONTENTS

ACKNOWLEDGMENTS

My deep thanks goes to those who helped me climb this mountain. God purposely placed you in my life, eliminating my need to search:

W	K	G	M	J	A	S	M	I	N	E	C	S
I	H	A	A	C	H	T	Q	V	K	B	G	H
L	R	Q	L	Z	L	E	L	J	I	D	E	A
L	L	X	C	D	Z	V	Y	U	U	S	S	R
I	T	Y	O	T	M	E	D	S	W	K	N	O
E	B	O	L	C	T	L	E	T	K	Z	I	N
&	U	R	M	P	K	U	U	I	N	D	L	W
K	J	G	J	E	A	K	O	N	X	I	P	I
A	Y	F	E	X	J	E	H	&	D	Q	S	L
T	K	Q	N	N	T	K	S	R	L	I	R	E
I	D	H	K	G	E	N	B	O	C	S	T	S
E	J	X	I	F	T	G	K	B	V	K	H	T
G	N	F	N	T	O	P	R	B	C	W	F	G
R	L	M	S	D	U	Q	D	I	U	B	O	Z
O	O	N	H	A	D	S	H	E	F	I	D	K
V	Y	T	L	O	W	A	Q	K	U	F	B	E
E	U	T	P	F	K	B	I	E	L	V	I	R
E	S	I	O	E	D	E	N	I	S	E	U	N

INTRODUCTION

"Good Morning!"

More than just a positive statement about a certain time of day, "Good Morning" is a feeling and attitude. One of the best feelings is when I awake first thing in the morning with my mind and body filled with positive energy. When I can climb out of bed with a smile, knowing the day is going to be good and that I have total control over it, it is a feeling like no other. Often times, no matter what time of day, I tell myself and others, "Good Morning," to share that special feeling.

"Good Morning" has very little to do with this book, yet at the same time, it has everything to do with this book. This book is about altering your mindset. It is intended to remind you that no matter the situation, you have control over what happens next. But it all starts with your attitude and frame of mind. One of my favorite quotes from Charles Swindoll is, *"Life is ten percent what happens to you and ninety percent how you react to it."*

"Beep, beep, beep . . ."

That's your alarm clock. It is time to wake up, climb out of bed, put a smile on your face, seize the day, and take control of your life.

I hope you enjoy.

Chapter One
NINE-YEAR-OLD KING

"Let me win, but if I cannot win, let me be brave in the attempt."

–Special Olympics Prayer

W [illegible]rite childhood game called "King of the Hill." Despite the name of the game, we never played on an actual hill. We used any makeshift platform or surface which boasted even the slightest elevation.

One particularly hot summer day, my neighbor's porch happened to be the "hill." For those not familiar with the game, it is played with much physicality, mainly consisting of pushing and shoving. To become king you must endure and withstand all forces to be the lone person standing on top of the hill. One of the best characteristics about King of the Hill is the king usually doesn't stay king for long. Someone eventually musters enough strength to get off the ground, charge back to the hill, and dethrone whoever is king and crown themselves. Those who possess enough will and determination usually become king at one time or another.

I shoved, they pushed; I pushed and they shoved, just as three young rough and energetic boys should. I had been crowned king five times. Even as a youngster, the feeling of being king, being successful and superior, couldn't be matched.

As the air grew warmer, we took a break. Ti-Juan, Orie, and I flopped down on the porch. As our panting calmed, we talked. The conversation started out as it always did between Ti-Juan and me, both of us proclaiming and defending ourselves as being the better athlete. Orie was the tallest of us three, but he never entered the best athlete dispute. His talents did not include athleticism. After a few minutes of self glory, the conversation turned to me and Ti-Juan saying we were going to play professional basketball and be on the same NBA team.

"I'm going to play for the Bulls," I shouted as I threw up my hands as if I were shooting a basket. It was the era of the great Michael Jordan in the 90s, who led the Chicago Bulls to six championships.

"Me, too," yelled Ti-Juan.

Just as the conversation reached the point where we were verbally dreaming of winning an NBA Championship, Orie's dad came out of the house and sat on the porch. The presence of Orie's dad made us lower our voices as if we were in trouble. Orie's dad was mean. He was erratic; you never knew what you were going to get with him. One day he would seem warm and kind, and the next you would think he was Satan in the flesh.

"You boys havin' fun?" Orie's dad asked.

"Yes, sir," we replied.

"Y'all come over here; I want to talk to you."

As we gathered around, Orie's dad said, "Tell me what y'all wanna be when y'all grow up." He looked to his son first and waited for his response.

"Um, I want to be a doctor," Orie stated after hesitating.

"That's good, son."

Without hesitation, Ti-Juan piped up, a childish smirk on his face. "I'm going to be an NBA player—the best ever!"

"An NBA player, huh? That's one hell of a dream there Ti-Juan."

Then it was my turn. It took me a little longer to respond than the others because I couldn't decide on what I wanted most: to be an NBA player or a lawyer. Since I didn't want to be like Ti-Juan and say an NBA player, I said with confidence,

"I'm going to be a lawyer."

There was a pause of uncomfortable silence. Orie's dad looked me square in the eye and replied, "You ain't gonna be nothin', boy!"

I was nine years old, told by an adult that I would become a failure. That I was a failure. That my dream would never be achieved.

Words like that aren't something you ever forget. Spoken at such an impressionable age, such words have the power to permanently damage a young mind or to become self-fulfilling prophecy.

I bolted off the porch as my eyes filled with tears and my heart with anger. After running a few yards I turned back to give Orie's dad a piece of my mind. I was choked up so no words came out, but I managed to illustrate my thoughts with an appropriate hand gesture. I know two wrongs don't make a right and I was always taught to respect my elders, but my actions at the time seemed necessary. Not just as a retaliation factor, but as a confidence builder that I was going to push back against any forces that tried to take me down.

An unexplainable emotion ran through my heart that day: I knew I was going to be the exact opposite of what Orie's dad told me. I was going to be something.

Chapter Two
WTF

"Only those who dare to fail greatly can ever achieve greatly."

–Robert F. Kennedy

If you were posed the question, *Are you waiting to succeed or fail in life?* how would you answer? Most people will answer that they're waiting to succeed. After all, not everyone is a Mark Zuckerberg, who at age twenty co-created Facebook, one of the most popular web-based programs ever which is used by millions of people. Not everyone makes it big at such an early age. Most people work hard for years to achieve their goals and dreams, or, like some business entrepreneurs, hustle to make a million, lose it all (sometimes more than once), and then make another million. Most people are waiting for success to find them.

Up until recently, I would have said I was waiting to succeed. For years I waited on success, confident it could come at any time. The experience I had at age nine with my neighbor's father telling me I wasn't going to be anything was something I never forgot. His words were utterly inappropriate, yet they helped shape me to what I soon would become. Knowing that at least one person envisioned me failing made me want to prove not only to him, but to the world, that I would succeed.

It's not as if I had an easy life or was born with a silver spoon in my mouth which made success easier to achieve. The odds have always been stacked against me. I was born two months premature and lived the first six weeks of my life in an incubator. Baby pictures of me in the hospital show me dependent on respirators, monitoring machines and all sorts of other medical equipment. Yet contrary to being weak or inheriting one of the many health complications to which preemies are at risk, I was strong. So strong, in fact, one photo captures me ripping the taped medical tubes off my face. I was not old enough to be out of the hospital, yet I was ready to take on the world.

From academics to athletics, from high school through college, in my private and business life, I waited on success. And waited. And waited. I worked hard, worked overtime, set goals, improved my skill set, talked with the right people, and yet I was still *waiting*.

At every stage of my life, there was always someone who believed I would fail. Neighbors, teachers, coaches, and even society anticipated my failure (predictions about African-Americans coming from similar neighborhoods and backgrounds as mine does not often scream success). I was aware of their anticipation of my imminent failure—but it only increased my determination to succeed.

It wasn't until after twenty-seven years of waiting on success that it dawned on me I had the wrong mindset concerning success and failure. I realized the expectations of me failing actually allowed me not to be afraid to fail. No matter what I faced, I wasn't afraid to fall on my face and get back up again.

Unfortunately, many people have the exact opposite frame of mind and are afraid of failing. Some are so terrified that they view any form of failing as negative, while few don't even try to succeed just to avoid any potential failure.

Through my experiences, I've learned failing can be positive as well as advantageous. Success doesn't mean the absence of failure, just as failure doesn't mean the lack of success. Failure itself can actually be a stepping stone to success. One of the greatest positives of failing is you are able to eliminate that failure as a possible route to success and move on to the next potential solution. Much like getting the education for a career choice and then finding out you don't like doing that job after all, you determine what is really most important to you for fulfillment and then you switch careers.

While the phrase *waiting to fail* may be misinterpreted as waiting for the inevitable, unavoidable failure, you may discover that it possesses a much deeper concept and outlook.

Here's how: the definition of *wait* means *to postpone or delay something, or to be postponed or delayed.* If you are waiting to succeed, you are postponing success. Similarly, if you are waiting to fail, you are postponing failure. I would much rather postpone the latter. Keep in mind there is no time limit on postponement. Who's to say it won't last forever? I have known things to be postponed so long that they never happen.

Also, if you are waiting to fail, you have ample time to prepare for it if it does occur. Again, some people don't want to associate with failure, so they don't think about it or prepare themselves for it. This irony is best described by Benjamin Franklin: *"By failing to prepare, you are preparing to fail."*

The purpose of this book is to show you how waiting to fail can be your road to success. Waiting to succeed versus waiting to fail is simply a mindset which can be changed so that you escape from the vicious cycle of perpetual waiting for success. I am waiting to fail. If it never happens, great; if it does, I'll be ready for it. In the meantime, while I am waiting to fail, I'll be busy succeeding. Call it reverse psychology, but I call it a blueprint for winning, a blueprint which can be applied to relationships, education, career, finances, and even religious beliefs.

So, are you waiting to succeed or waiting to fail?

Chapter Three

CRACKED LIFE

"Life consists not in holding good cards, but in playing well those you hold."

–Josh Billings

Growing up, I didn't have a relationship with my father. I was two years old when he left. Unsatisfied with his job with the U.S. Post Office and longing for a fresh start in a different state, he moved from Ohio to California. His intentions were good and his plan seemed flawless; he would move, find work and then move my mother and I. I at least know he got the first part right. My father did move to California, but weeks passed and there was no word from him. My mother knew something was wrong. It wasn't in his character to disappear and default on his responsibilities. At least she thought so.

Another month or so passed without anyone knowing my father's whereabouts, condition or anything. And then one day the telephone rang. The voice on the other end said, "You have a collect call from a federal correctional facility, do you accept the charges?" My father was in jail. He got caught up with the wrong crowd. His thoughts of securing a job after his arrival to California didn't happen as quickly or as seamless as he hoped. Meanwhile, crack cocaine was on the rise in the mid 1980s, so my father sold it to make money. I guess he thought distributing drugs was just as easy as distributing mail. He was wrong. He was arrested three weeks after his move. His guilt and shame kept him from notifying us right away.

My father was sentenced to six months jail time. After he was released, his probation required he stay within the state of California for two years. I'm not sure what happened within those two years, but he never returned home. He didn't call or write. My mother later heard he went back to dealing crack cocaine and eventually started using it. All communication was severed.

Not having my father was a non-issue initially. I was too young to understand and between my mother, grandparents and aunt, I had all the love a kid could need. Then a tragic accident changed the dynamics of my world. My grandfather died. He was helping cut down a neighbor's tree and took a tragic blow to the head by a branch. My grandfather's death delivered a crushing blow to my mother's mental state. Adding to the fact that she was young and raising a child by herself, she lost the person she was closest to. She couldn't handle it.

My mother began to take her anger and frustration out on herself. Drinking and partying was her way of escaping and masking the pain. It wasn't long before the drinking lead to the use of social drugs. One high lead to another, then another high was needed to keep from coming down from the previous. She became dependent. Her drug of choice was crack cocaine.

My mother and I moved a lot, but we always stayed in close proximity to my grandmother. My mother knew if my grandmother was close by, she would watch and take care of me, which my mother took advantage of. Frequent late nights, overnights, and sometimes multiple days of binging often found me in my grandmother's care. Not only did I not have a father, but I eventually became second to drugs as being the most important thing in my mother's life.

One morning I awoke and the apartment was quiet. I climbed out of bed and searched upstairs but found no one. Downstairs was the same as I walked through the living room to the kitchen. I opened the refrigerator and lugged out a half-gallon milk carton. Luckily, it was only half full and my four year-old body could handle it. What my body couldn't handle was my mouth being filled with curled, chunky, spoiled milk. The spoiled milk upset my stomach—and me.

I got scared. I ran to the back door and tried to open it. The locks on the door where made so that you needed a key for both the outside and inside. I ran to the front door. Again, due to the locks I was unable to open it. A feeling of abandonment overwhelmed me and I screamed and cried. My only thought was to escape. Our front door had two-inch square windowpanes. I reached back and punched the glass as hard as I could. I did it again and again. Finally, the glass broke. Without thinking, I tried to stick my head through the opening. After realizing my head was too big and there was no way I was getting out, I yelled, "Help! Help! Mom! Grandma!"

After about ten minutes of yelling, tears and cries for help, my mother came rushing through the door.

"Oh my God, what happened to you?" She noticed my bloody hand from busting the window. "Let's get you cleaned up. Everything's going to be all right."

My mother said everything was going to be all right, but it wasn't. My grandmother lived six houses down the street and that's where she said she was. But it didn't matter where she was; it wasn't the first or last time she wasn't around when I needed her.

In time, my mother's drug habit became worse. I often saw people in and out of our apartment whom I didn't know. Sometimes I even witnessed her getting high. It wasn't a positive environment for me. With no other option to turn to, my grandmother eventually took matters into her own hands by calling the local authorities. They took me out of my mother's care and placed me with my grandmother at age five.

Sidebar I credit my grandmother for helping make me the man I am today. In fact, my grandmother and family were the dominant influences in my life while growing up.

The relationships developed throughout our lives play a significant role in our direction and development, both emotionally and spiritually and career-wise. Our relationship with God, parents, siblings, partners, children, extended family, friends, co-workers, and even our enemies have a direct correlation on how we think, speak, and act. Just think how different your life would be if some of the relationships you have were non-existent, both the ones bestowed on you and the ones you've chosen, or think how different your life would be if you developed a relationship with whom you don't already have a connection. See what I mean about those relationships playing a significant role?

We often overlook the depth of relationships and how they ultimately affect us both in the short and long term. Relationships affect us in positive and negative ways. It is important to distance yourself from relationships which have a negative impact on your life, even if it is close friends or family, and strengthen those which are positive (I am sure you have probably heard that once or twice before). When I was younger, my grandmother would strongly suggest whom I should and shouldn't hang out with. Of course back then I didn't take heed to her suggestions since I didn't fully respect the power of influence. Now that I am older and wiser, I understand which relationships will help propel me forward and which will hinder my progression.

At this point of my life, I not only try to develop relationships and surround myself with people who are like-minded, but who are also smarter and more successful than I am. If you are the smartest person in your circle, then you are limiting your growth.

Perhaps one of the most significant relationships two human beings can have is the parent-child relationship. It is important that fear of failure does not exist in it. Due to the lack of relationship with my father and the dysfunctional relationship I had with my mother, I often wonder how I will be as a father and a parent. Although I have promised myself that I will one day be the father to my child that I never had, there are times when I ask, "Will my parenting be good enough?" I know I am not alone in thinking this way because I have actually heard others ask similar questions such as, "Am I a bad parent?" or "Did I fail as a parent?"

It seems far too often that parents are not responsible and mature, or are trying to be more of a friend to their children than an actual parent. In some cases, parents have no regard for their children and abandon them to their grandparents. Others had a harsh upbringing; justifiably, they do everything they can to make their child's life easier. Then there are cases where there is only one parent raising the child and they try to overcompensate to provide a sense of balance.

Yet there are no rulebooks for parenting. I am sure there are people out there that wish they could turn to section III, page 927 of a book and find out what to do when their six year-old decides to take the family car for a spin and crashes into a light pole. Now that scenario may be a little far fetched for most, but don't act like that hasn't happened before. What I am getting at is that each parent handles their child differently and some have a fear of applying certain methods that they feel may damper the relationship between them and their child. Although the sense of failing as a parent can come from both ends of the spectrum of being too hard or too soft, it seems that more and more people are shying away from applying what our elders might consider appropriate discipline.

I don't have any children, but I don't believe one has to have a child to see the direction our youth are heading, of which I see enough evidence through my various appearances and visits to schools and youth programs. There are an abundance of kids who simply don't care about anything and are not afraid of anything. I blame their parents and upbringing, though it is still up to each kid to overcome the deficiencies of that upbringing to succeed in life.

It all goes back to what I mentioned earlier, how a person thinks and what they say and do is directly related to their relationships with others. The first relationship a child has is with their parents or caregiver. From that day forth, it's up to that parent to teach that child and direct them in the way they should go.

Notice I said the way they should go, not the way they want to go. Children often want things and want to do things which are not good for them or in their best interest. Again, it's up to the parents to not give in, to stand their ground for what they know is right.

Children are smart; they will test the limits to see what they can get away with. They start off small, seeing if they can get away with staying up past their bedtime and pitching a fit until their parents give in to their demands. Once they have their parents cowed at an early age, they can continue to bully them through childhood, adolescence, and on through adulthood—all because the parents would not put their foot down about unacceptable behavior.

It is said what a child is like in childhood, they'll be like as a teenager. Imagine what a spoiled six year-old will turn into at age sixteen—pouting will turn to shouting; tantrums will turn to damaging property; stealing a quarter out of the ashtray escalates into stealing merchandise out of the mall. On the flip side, a child who is taught to respect their elders, to center their life on positive things and steer clear of negative influences, will be a teenager and later an adult who knows how to control themselves and how to work hard to succeed.

My challenge to every parent reading this is try not to get overly consumed with being a likeable parent, but instead focus on being a respected parent. Be the model for the behavior you want your kids to exhibit. I am not implying that it is not important to be liked by your children; but the truth of the matter is, regardless of how hard you try, there are going to be days when your children will not be so fond of you. But there should never be a day when you are not respected as a mother or father.

Chapter Four

THIEVES, BULLIES & NERDS

"The best armor is to keep out of reach."

–Italian Proverb

I grew up on the north side of Columbus, Ohio. The neighborhood I was raised in wasn't the worst, but it sure wasn't the best. Similar to most lower-to-middle class neighborhoods, I was surrounded by drugs, gangs and violence. Police helicopters and sirens filled the air on a regular basis. Seeing prostitutes on my walk to school was normal, while passing dealers at the corner store on the walk home from school was standard. Many negative outside influences were present and it was real easy to get caught up doing the wrong thing at a young age.

Stealing was one of the more popular things to do. I tried it once and got caught. It wasn't even anything big. I tried stealing some candy from a store in the mall. My grandmother noticed I had something in my hand that she didn't buy. She made me go back to the store, return it and apologize. She was so stern and I was so afraid that I thought, "Never again."

There was one other thing back in my day that kids stole outside of the normal thefts of candy and bikes. It was a popular line of coats called Starter jackets. They were designed to match the color and logos of professional sports teams. You weren't cool if you didn't have a Starter. They were in such high demand that kids were literally beating people up and taking them right off their backs. I had two of them. One was a Chicago Bulls pullover, my favorite, and the other was a Dallas Cowboys zip up. I was prepared to put up a fight if someone tried to steal mine. It got so bad that I started carrying a knife to school when I wore my jacket, just in case.

Even with all the negative neighborhood influences, the positive influence I received at home was far greater. It was centered on God. Church was a must. Whether I wanted to go or not, my grandmother would make me. She made me go even when she didn't. She would arrange for the church bus to pick me up, and tell Mr. Walker, the driver, to look after me. The values which my grandmother instilled in me at a very early age played a vital part in me not becoming a statistic. Because she stood her ground, enforced rules, and commanded respect, I stayed out of trouble and am a better adult today.

Coupling my not- afraid-to-fail attitude with the mindset of not wanting to be like my mother or father, yielded a school-aged kid knowing he had to rise above his surroundings and be better than what was customary to reach success. Considering I was in elementary school, the type of success and how I would rise to success was still yet to be determined. The only success I could relate to back then was to be rich. I saw poor people and I saw people I thought were rich. I wanted to emulate the latter. I figured the best way to become rich and achieve success was to strive to be the best and not follow what everyone else did.

My first test in this was school. Just as it is now in some places, it wasn't cool to be smart back then. In fact, the worse you did in school, the more respect you got from your peers. But that went against my notion of being the best, so while my classmates went out of their way to be cool under-achievers, I focused on the opposite. I didn't know where getting good grades would lead me, but I figured it was the one thing I could control. I had no control over my birth, my parents or the way I was raised, but I could control my learning.

I paid the price with regard to my decision to learn. I was often teased throughout grade school for being smart. Being called a nerd was normal. It was also upsetting. The reality was that school was easy for me. I never went through extraordinary lengths to get good grades. I just went to school, paid attention, and the rest followed. Ironically, I had some friends that were just as smart as I was; they just didn't apply themselves. Justifiably, in their minds, they may have not had any reason to, as there was rarely any talk about college or a higher education amongst them or in their homes.

Despite doing well in school, I had no thoughts about college either. Not once did I think I would attend. It wasn't a lack of aspiration but a lack of knowledge. I don't know at what point the thought of college enters a kid's mind, so maybe I was just too young, but I do know at one point I didn't think I would live past the age of twenty-one. There simply was no rationale to think about college when you didn't think you'd be alive to go.

I eventually grew out of the nerd thing as people started accepting me for who I was. Playing sports also helped balance my social experiences. I played a variety of sports, but football and basketball were my favorite by far. It was about the third grade when I realized my true athleticism. During recess I would play football. Carrying the same last name as Emmitt Smith, the Hall of Fame running back who played for the Dallas Cowboys, only boosted my ego. Imitating him, I would always be the ball carrier. Before the play, I would announce to the defense the direction I was going and exactly which moves I was going to do on the upcoming play. I would take the handoff, do just as I had anticipated, and score.

I was virtually unstoppable—at least at recess I was. My playground antics didn't go over so well in my early days of playing on an organized team. I played for several little league football teams, but I remember one team in particular, the Northside Bulldogs. Being one of the younger players on the team, they didn't value my potential one bit. I was told I was too small. I hardly got any playing time during my first season, which led to several instances of me going home after the game crying and upset. But the disappointments I experienced with sports at an early age taught me how to handle and overcome adversity. It was a substitute for the fatherly advice I missed. Growing up in a household with just my grandmother around, I had to learn and grow from every experience. I had to essentially teach myself how to be a young man, which included self-teachings of the typical father-son activities like throwing a football, shooting a basketball and catching a baseball.

I even learned how to handle a gun on my own. In fourth grade, my grandmother's job relocated her to Circleville, Ohio. Circleville is a good forty-five minute drive from Columbus. To add insult to the already long drive, my grandmother had to drive at night because she worked the good ol' 10p.m.-7a.m. graveyard shift. That left me at home alone. Some people may view this as neglect. I didn't. I saw it as my grandmother doing what she had to do to provide for us.

One Thursday night, she kissed me on the cheek before she left for work and told me I could stay up until 10 o'clock to finish watching my favorite show, *New York Undercover*. I loved that show. It was shows like that and movies like *In Too Deep* which made me want to be an undercover cop. Still to this day, I fantasize about being one. As the show ended, I did just as my grandmother said by turning off the television and going to bed. Bright moonlight and breezes rattling the windows kept me awake. Then a noise downstairs heightened my senses. I slowly got out of bed and tiptoed to my grandmother's room.

Adrenaline coursing through my body, I felt I could hear and smell everything. The noise seemed to grow louder. I opened my grandmother's armoire where she kept her gun. I rifled through a few shirts and pulled out her black .38 caliber snub-nosed pistol. As I made my way to the hallway pistol in hand, I mulled over my two options: go after them or let them come after me.

I ran down the stairs cursing and screaming as loud as I could. "Y'all muthafucka's better get out my house or I'm gonna blow your brains out!" I switched on every light and cleared each room just like Eddie Torres and J.C. Williams did in *New York Undercover*. After searching the entire house, I realized no one was there and the noise must have been a figment of my imagination.

I returned upstairs and put the gun back just as I had found it. I went back to my room and climbed in bed. Despite my foul language and tough guy act, I thanked the Lord for not letting anyone be in the house. I still had reservations about the noise, so I checked under my pillow to make sure my BB gun was there. It's imperative to have a plan B.

My grandmother only had to drive to Circleville for a couple more years, as she retired soon thereafter. I no longer had to stay in the house at night by myself, but by that time I was in middle school and I actually wanted to be home alone. The noises didn't scare me so much once puberty kicked in. In fact, once puberty kicked in, not much frighten me at all. I had started to gain that physical and mental confidence and toughness that most boys seek. Then I was put to the test.

I was in seventh grade. A guy by the name of Wayne Kelso had just enrolled. It was already midway through the school year and word around school was Wayne was sent to my school because of his past expulsions at other schools and his recent stint at the juvenile detention home. Wayne and I had gym class together his first day. We were playing kickball. I remember rounding second base and heading to third when I noticed Wayne in my way. I jumped over him, hit third base and made it to home plate scoring a run. After my run, Wayne came charging at me with the ball, mad because I jumped over him. I thought he was playing so I dodged his throw and ran out the gym as the class bell rang.

As the weeks progressed I became aware that Wayne wasn't playing; he had some sort of grievance against me. He would make intimidating gestures in class and in the hallways. I ignored his antagonism, mainly because I knew he had friends and relatives that I didn't want conflict with. Being I didn't have any brothers, cousins, or male figures in my life to go to battle with me, I had to make sure my encounters were on a one-on-one basis.

After awhile, enough was enough. I decided the next time Wayne gave me a look or said something slick, it was going to come to blows. I envisioned the fight in my head several times. My imaginary scene took place in the gym locker room:

Wayne always had a lollipop in his mouth, so I struck first, aiming directly at the lollipop with the palm of my hand, jamming the candy down his throat. Ooh's and aah's from the other students in the locker room did not distract my charge or keep me from ramming Wayne into the lockers, toppling them like dominoes. I taught Wayne a quick lesson which assured he would think twice the next time he tried to bully someone.

And a dream it was, as our next real encounter didn't quite play out like that. I was on my way home from school after a long day of soccer practice. With my neighborhood designed in a typical grid fashion, there were various ways to walk home. For some reason that day I cut down a side street I rarely traveled, and guess who I ran into? Wayne Kelso. He wasn't by himself, either, so I knew there was going to be trouble. He and his buddy stood on the corner starring and whispering as I approached.

"What you doing walking down this street?"

"Walking home."

"I told you the next time I saw you it was going to be trouble."

I tried to cross the street to avoid them, but Wayne's friend yelled, "Get him." They ran towards me and I took off. They chased me for a couple blocks but I cut through houses, hopped a couple of fences, and lost them. As soon as I got home, I told my grandmother. She was furious. She called downtown and we eventually went to court over the matter. By the time our court date arrived, Wayne was already in custody for another offense. I don't recall the outcome of our court hearing, but I didn't see Wayne again until years later.

Another test of my toughness came in the eighth grade. Ricky and me were shooting basketball at a nearby school. Dusk was approaching and the adjacent field behind us became darker. As we were shooting around, I instinctively looked to the field and asked Ricky if he saw something move. Unfazed, Ricky kept shooting. Minutes later I swore I had seen something move in the field again. I thought I was tripping. The next thing I knew, as I was shooting a free throw, a guy dressed in all black ran up on us with his gun drawn. I took off running and before the ball hit the ground I swear I was on the other side of the building. Poor Ricky didn't react fast enough and got left behind with the gunman. As tough as I thought I was before, I didn't dare go back around the other side of the building. I spotted a couple of people in the parking lot and pleaded to them that my friend was on the other side being held up. They were very timid and hesitant to help. Looking back, I probably would've been the same way. Eventually, I got a gentleman to escort me back around the building to check on my friend. When I turned the corner, there was Ricky all by himself. I couldn't believe he hadn't been harmed. He was shook up, but luckily for him the guy who ran up on us happened to be some sort of distant relative. He told Ricky he was on his way to rob a convenient store. He also told him to tell me I was a punk for running.

Losers will try to make you feel like a loser no matter what choice you make. If I had stayed with Ricky, his relative might have robbed me or I might have been shot. Now which choice seems like the losing choice? Run to safety or stay and get shot?

Chapter Five
NBA OR NFL

"Character cannot be developed in ease and quiet. Only through experience of trial and suffering can the soul be strengthened, vision cleared, ambition inspired, and success achieved."

–Helen Keller

I endured many tests and challenges throughout middle school and could only imagine what experiences were ahead at the high school level. Moving on to high school felt like such a big feat. I had the opportunity to choose what school I wanted to attend, which was a pretty daunting task. I had three criteria which my chosen school needed to satisfy: a good curriculum, a good sports program, and a good selection of hot girls.

Many of the city schools failed to comply in one area or another, but I did find some promise in Beechcroft High School. Beechcroft was somewhat of a distance from where I lived, so not many kids in my neighborhood decided to go there. Many went to Linden McKinley, which was just a few blocks from my house, while some chose to drop out. One of which was Ti-Juan. Despite our big dreams of one day playing on the same NBA team together, Ti-Juan decided the street life was more important. He got caught up. He started selling weed our eighth grade year and put school on the back burner.

The first time I saw Ti-Juan dealing drugs, I teared up. I knew school wasn't his forte, but when I saw him pull a small bag of weed out of his shorts and slap it across another guys hand for the exchange of a Hamilton, I knew it was a wrap. Even though Ti-Juan was content with being in the streets, I was determined to live out the dreams we once had of making it to the pros.

Every year I seemed to toggle between football and basketball as my favorite sport, but at the start of high school I was on a basketball high, so much so that I decided to only play basketball my freshman year. I spent the first couple of months of high school enjoying myself and getting acclimated to my new school, but as basketball season approached, I began a consistent practice regimen. I would practice in the alley behind my house with my portable hoop. I would practice dribbling and shooting with my right hand, then my left. I would work on all my moves. I even gave all my signature moves nicknames.

Basketball tryouts arrived and I was ready. I remember that day so vividly. I caught the bus to Beechcroft on a crisp Saturday morning. My yellow Walkman was blaring Jay-Z's *Vol. 2 Hard Knock Life* as I walked from the bus stop to the school. I was pumped. The gym was full of eager athletes ready to display their talent. After everyone changed into their basketball attire, the coach explained the tryouts. It was to be a two-day tryout, day one consisting of fundamental drills and day two consisting of pick up games.

Tryouts started with a lay-up drill. My first couple attempts at the basket were good. Then I noticed some guys in front of me being a little stylish as they attempted their shots. One style in particular we called "smacking board." At the time I was approximately 5'7" and just learned to smack boards. Not to be outdone by the competition, I tried to get a little stylish on my next several attempts. I think I missed all but one. The next drill was a shooting drill. Players shot from various positions on the court. I performed better in this drill, but still not as good as I hoped. We played mini games for the final drill of the day. I was pretty happy with my play. I felt I could have done a little better earlier in the tryouts, but I would be able to make up and prove myself on day two. Afterward, the coach revealed that there would be no second day and all cuts and decisions would be based on how we performed that day. I was bummed.

A week or so after tryouts, the coach put up the list of those who made the squad. Everybody who tried out ran to the door to search for their name. My heart was racing as I approached the board. As the crowd cleared a bit, I scanned the list, first looking for Smith. I couldn't find it. Thinking the list may have been sorted by first names, I searched for Antonio. Again, no luck. Reality set in. I was so disappointed in myself, mainly because I knew my silly antics during the lay-up drill played a part in me not making the team. I couldn't believe all my hard work and practice didn't pay off.

As I said before, failure can be a stepping stone to success.

Not making the team my freshman year inspired me even more to make the team the next year. All I could think about was how Michael Jordan got cut from his basketball team as a sophomore and went on to become one of the greatest basketball players ever. I was determined to get some get back. As a matter of fact, I was so motivated that I decided that not only was I going to play basketball my sophomore year, I was going to play football, too. Little did I know, football would ultimately become my sport of choice. It just goes to show you that although many people view failure in a negative light, it often brings out the positive and shows you a different direction to take that can ultimately lead to success.

By the time my sophomore year hit, I pretty much had the high school routine figured out. My promise to myself was to play football that year and I did. It was a lot different from the little league football I was used to playing in the years prior. There was weightlifting, summer training, and of course two-a-day practices. It was tough. It took me the entire summer and the first couple of games to find my groove, but by mid-season I became dominant. I didn't even play offense and averaged one touchdown per game. I was an interception machine. Everyone knew if I caught the ball that six points where going on the scoreboard. Did I mention it was junior varsity?

For me, playing sports equaled popularity. The attention I got my sophomore year quadrupled from what I received a year earlier. My confidence went through the roof. I started dressing a little nicer and grooming myself a little better. I even put an s-curl in my hair to change up my look. I remember walking through the halls one day and a girl told me I looked like Detective Torres from *New York Undercover* with my curl. I didn't know if the comment was good or bad, but how ironic. It was my favorite show growing up but Torres wasn't exactly the look I was going for. Yet with curly hair and a name like Antonio, I guess you can't help but have a little Spanish flare.

Basketball season started just as football season ended. I worked extremely hard during my time off to improve my game. I wasn't sure if I would make the team, but I knew one thing; I wasn't going to make the same mistakes as I had the previous year. The same progression of tryouts and waiting for the final cut list took place my sophomore year, but unlike the previous year, the announcement of who made the team was delivered in a very suspenseful, atypical fashion. Instead of posting the list, the coach actually went to each room and handed the players who made the team their uniform.

When our classroom door opened and the basketball coach entered our room, jerseys in hand, I stopped breathing. After a brief conversation with the teacher, the coach proceeded down the aisles of the room. There were several students who had tried out for the team in my class. I was sitting in the back of the room. As the coach made his way toward my direction, he stopped midway in the aisle and handed one of my good friends his jersey. Smiles, claps and congratulations were in order. My nervousness and anxiety rose to the max. The coach then turned and started walking back towards the front of the room. *Damn it*, I thought to myself. I didn't make the cut again. Then the coach turned back as if he had some unfinished business. He walked to the back of the room and handed me a jersey. "Welcome to the team," he said.

My hard work, discipline and dedication had paid off. It was such a great feeling to turn a once-failed situation into success.

Although most of that basketball season is now a blur, there is one game I will never forget. It sticks out the most because it happened to be the only game of the season in which I didn't step on the court. It was my punishment for being a few minutes late to one of our game day warm-ups. For starters, I was so close to being on time, I didn't even realize my coach knew I was late until he told me at halftime. Secondly, I had a good excuse. "See, what had happened was . . ."

Isn't that how excuses usually start out? I had gone to my mother's house after school because she was supposed to take me to get my temporary driver's permit that day. Don't ask me why I picked the day of a basketball game to go, but I was eager to get my permit. When I got to my mother's house, she wasn't there. I didn't know that initially, as I thought she might have been in the house sleeping off her high or drunkenness, which was not uncommon. I didn't have a key to her house, but I didn't need one as I had my own secret entrance of climbing through her upstairs bathroom window. I made my way up the house, climbed through the window, and once inside realized that she really wasn't there. I called everyone I could think of trying to find her whereabouts. We had planned and talked about that day several times, so I just knew she would return home soon.

After waiting and waiting, I concluded that I wasn't going to get my permit that day and if I didn't head back to school I was going to miss my game. My only option was to catch the bus, which I knew would make me late. Since I had no other choice, I headed to the bus stop and waited. As luck would have it, while I was waiting for the bus, one of my cousins spotted me while driving by. She picked me up and rushed me to school. I thought I snuck into the gym without anyone noticing my tardiness. I tried telling the coach the story at halftime, thinking he would overturn his decision of not playing me. He listened and said he understood, but he still didn't play me.

A few years ago, while sitting in a meeting, I noticed a plaque on the wall which hit home with this situation and many others I faced. It read, "No Excuses, No Exceptions, Only Execution, And Expectations." I was angry that I didn't play that game, but looking back, I know the coach did the right thing.

After basketball season ended, track was next up on the agenda. Since I had missed out on playing sports my freshman year, it only made sense to make it up by playing as many sports as I could my sophomore year. Track was also great preparation for the next football season. The great thing about track is there weren't any cuts. If you were a fast runner, the coaches placed you in the sprinting events. If you weren't a fast runner, the coaches placed you in the long distance events. And if you couldn't run at all, you likely ended up throwing the discus or shot put. Either way, you made the team.

My challenge came not in making the general team, but making the 4x1 relay team. There were a few upper-classmen claiming their spots on the 4x1 relay team, as they had been a part of the team the year prior. Not to be intimidated, I threw my name in the mix. After weeks of grueling practice and competition, I got the nod to lead off the first leg of our 4x1 relay team in our first track meet and the rest of the season.

My sophomore year was a great year. It was a break-out year for me as I gained popularity, made a few female acquaintances, and of course made my mark in sports. My expectations for my junior year grew in all areas. One reason for my expected growth was the fact that I got a car the summer before my junior year. I got a 1992 maroon Hyundai Sonata. I dared anyone to call it purple. I was so excited. I got the car before I even got my license. I was in Driver's Education at the time. The funny thing was, I was the only student who drove to Driver's Ed class. I parked a block or two away and walk the rest so no one would see me.

A few years ago, there was a popular television show called *Pimp My Ride* where they would trick out a normal vehicle by equipping it with a whole bunch of expensive accessories like rims, TV's and custom paint jobs. I tried to mimic the show as best as I could with my car. I did away with the factory tires and got myself a set of 16" alloy rims. I kept them clean, too. I mounted a TV in the dash, and hooked up a DVD player and a Sony Playstation. You couldn't tell me nothin'. I even tried to self-tint the windows. That didn't turn out quite as I expected. My dumb self applied the tint on the outside of the windows instead of the inside. The tint lasted until the next rain. But I loved my first car.

It would later get me into trouble.

Chapter Six

FRICTIONLESS ROLLERCOASTER

"You have two choices in life: You can dissolve into the mainstream or you can be distinct. To be distinct you must be different. To be different, you must strive to be what no one else but you can be."

-Anonymous

My junior year didn't begin the way I had anticipated, at least from a sports standpoint. Due to the fact that I excelled more in football than basketball, plus I realized I probably wouldn't reach 6'0", I decided I would only participate in football and track my last two years of school. I had high hopes that I would be one of the starting cornerbacks for our varsity team as a junior.

Once again, an adverse situation presented itself. Throughout the summer, I attended an educational program called Upward Bound. This program was a six-week course held about thirty miles north of Columbus at Ohio Wesleyan University. The program only allowed me to go home on the weekends, so there was no way I could attend the program and participate in summer workouts with the football team. I had talked this through with my defensive backs coach before I made the decision to attend the summer program. He understood and I was under the impression there would be no ramifications, but during my time away in the summer program, some coaching changes took place. The defensive backs coach who was knowledgeable about my situation went over to the offensive side of the ball and a new coach was appointed to my position. The new coach and I were unfamiliar with each other and his philosophy was if you don't show up, you don't play.

As the first game of the season got underway, I was nowhere on the field. In my mind I went from projected starter to not even playing. I had two options: continue to work hard or fold with disappointment. After a couple of weeks of persistence in practice, I finally made my way onto the field via special teams. I continued to bust my butt and by midway through the season I had elevated myself to playing on almost all of the special teams units and sparingly on defense. By the end of the season, I had once again proved hard work, discipline and dedication trumps adversity by becoming the starting cornerback for the remaining few games.

Although the way the football season ended left me on top, the roller coaster ride of my junior year continued as life at home became stressful. The relationship between my grandmother and me, since she raised me, was more of a mother-son relationship. She was never the sweet grandma that said, “Come here baby, let me bake you some cookies.” It was more like, “You better get your butt over here before I knock you into next week.” As I was becoming a young man, that type of authority just didn’t bode well with me. We clashed often. Having a car only added fuel to the fire and became one of our arguing points as I never could make curfew. I tried hard, but twelve o’clock just always seemed to come way too fast.

Another low on the roller coaster came when I started to disregard school rules. Up until this point I had rarely seen trouble in school with teachers or administration. Unfortunately, my good boy persona began to get skewed. Schoolwork was still not much of a problem for me as I continued to get A’s and B’s. My problem was my eagerness to leave school during the day, especially during my study hall period. The mall and several restaurants were close by which were always enticing options. On several occasions I got caught leaving or coming back to school late. After getting into enough trouble for leaving school during study hall, I no longer left school, but turned to another form of entertainment, which was gambling.

Gambling was another form of income. I had a job at Wal-Mart, but then, just as it is now, having multiple streams of revenue is the key. Playing cards, betting on basketball and shooting dice were among our typical forms of gambling. Little enforcement was done on the first two because generally no money was out in the open. I got really good at the card game "Tunk" and usually always walked away with more money in my pocket than I sat down with. That was generally the case until I played with the person who originally taught me how to play, which was a girl.

Shooting dice, however, was a big no-no. We had to be more discrete and get it in wherever and whenever we could: the locker room, the bathroom, even between the bleachers. I once got caught by the school officers shooting dice in the stairwell on what was supposed to be a restroom break. One officer came from the top of the stairs. We tried to run the other way, but another officer appeared at the bottom of the staircase. I got sent to the principal's office for that one. Snake eyes.

Other negative influences and pressures came into play my junior year. Some of the most common at that age are alcohol, drugs and sex. I was good on alcohol and drugs, as I did not smoke nor drink, but sex was a totally different story. Everybody was doing it or at least they claimed they were. It was a competition with most of my guy friends to see how many girls they could sleep with. Cats were spreading the word daily about their proud sexual encounters. By no means was I trying to compete with the guys who professed to have more than fifty partners or share ambiguous tales with listeners. My initiation into the world of sex was not even story worthy. As bad as it sounds, I don't even remember the name of the first person I had sex with. In fact, I don't even think I knew her name to begin with. I know, I know, disgusting right? I had met her only moments before. My friend and I strolled over to one of his chick's houses so they could have sex. While they went upstairs, I sat on the couch to watch TV. She must have told one of her friends to keep me company, because this girl came downstairs and sat with me. They didn't have cable, so we never did watch TV.

Afterward, I remember feeling slightly remorseful as I reflected on what I had just done. I had given in to peer pressure and was acting like everyone else. For most of my life I had tried to move to a different beat than what was normal, but at that moment, I felt I was no different than the next person. How could I defy the words of Orie's father if I couldn't separate myself from the commoners?

Sex became the magnifier of some problems I faced at home. When your mind is driven by a want or a pleasure, it doesn't operate in the manner it should. Things are forgotten, overlooked, and sometimes ignored. I definitely had my share of regretful decisions regarding sex, one of the most regretful being having sex in my grandmother's house. Coming in a close second would be leaving my damn paraphernalia on the floor after having sex in my grandmother's house. I think my grandmother suspected something due to my changes in behavior, but it took little investigation as she found an empty condom wrapper I left laying in my bedroom. This caused a deep hurt to my grandmother. The disappointment and anger she felt was revealed through much aggression towards me for a long time. In turn, her aggression caused a great deal of hostility in our relationship. Every minute situation posed the threat of turning into an explosive argument at any given moment.

I reached the point where I was tired of talking and arguing and decided to show everyone that I was hurting too. One night, after arguing with what seemed to be everyone in my family, I hopped in my car and sped away from my mother's house. I drove to a neighboring street where there were recently installed roundabouts. I gassed my Sonata and I took each roundabout as fast as I could, turning the steering wheel back and forth, trying to flip my car over. I had no interest in killing myself but I figured time in the hospital would alleviate some of the stress applied by my family. I was unsuccessful and can only credit God and His angels for watching over me. Although I was not trying to die, I would have had no control of the outcome had my vehicle flipped.

Despite the rough patches of my junior year, some highlights did occur. One of the brightest spots was my mother started getting her act together and kicking her crack cocaine addiction which had spanned fifteen years. She bore her fourth child, my brother, the year prior, which started her cleanse. But she was only able to maintain her sobriety after she gave her life to Christ. She became a devout Christian and a totally different person. There was finally hope that at least one of her children would be able to grow up without the pain and heartache that my sisters and I experienced due to her addiction. There were no more late nights wondering where she was or if she was safe, and the days of receiving phone calls from the county jail were gone. Best of all, I finally had the opportunity to build a healthy relationship between my mother and me.

With my junior year behind me, my senior year couldn't have had a better start. I decided not to attend Upward Bound and used my time attending several football camps held at various colleges. I was able to amass interest from numerous schools due to my performance at the camps. Letters from Division I colleges started pouring in and made me a believer that I could actually play at the next level.

Our first game of the season was as much of a confidence booster as any. It was a hyped up game with a cross-town foe, the Independence 76ers. You could hear the home crowd chanting "I-High" as we entered their stadium. Having home field provided no advantage to the 76ers as we dominated the game. I provided two interceptions and a forced fumble to our team win. Following that game, I received a letter from a recruiting coach at Bowling Green State University. After reading his praises of my play, I knew that I would eventually be offered a scholarship to become a Falcon. It was a worst-case scenario for me; my aspirations grew to play for a big-time school.

Sorry to say, my extraordinary play in the first game crippled my opportunities over the next several games. My two interceptions in Game One caused other opponents not to throw to my side of the field. I literally had two pass attempts to my side over the next three games.

Even though I was a non-factor, we were still winning games. In fact, we were blowing teams out by fifty and sixty points. By mid-season we were ranked the top team in the state and had accumulated 198 points to our opponents 14 through the first four games. My lack of work over the three-game span proved to be a crucial factor in our Game Five loss to our rival, Northland High School, on our homecoming night. It was the worst game our team and I ever played. I gave up two receptions to Northland's receivers, one of which was a touchdown. My team gave up eight or nine turnovers that night. We lost to a mediocre team that hadn't beaten us in almost twenty years.

As the regular season continued, we brushed off the fluke loss to Northland and regained our status as the top team in the state by season's end. Unfortunately the limited action I saw from our opponent's offenses caused a decrease in the interest and letters I received from colleges. Bowling Green seemed more and more like a favorable option. We ended the regular season with a record of 9-1, with six of the teams not scoring a single point against us. My interception tally rose to five as the regular season wrapped up.

Things were looking up. We made it to the playoffs with one of the best teams Beechcroft had in a while. We were always known to make it to the playoffs, but over the years we had problems winning a game. I experienced first round playoff loses in both my sophomore and junior year. Our main focus was to beat our first round opponent. With a final score of 7-6, we did just that. It was a hard- fought battle with our city league opponent, Walnut Ridge, but we came out victorious. It was our school's first playoff win in ten years.

Our second round opponent proved to be an even greater challenge. We played a dominant first half of football, leading New Carlisle Tecumseh 13-0 at halftime. I remember going into the locker room at halftime and joking with teammates of how great our next game was going to be. Teams which made it to the third round were to play at the Columbus Crew stadium, the home of Columbus' professional soccer team. We were excited to play on such a big stage.

When we came out of the locker room for the second half of the game, we noticed most of our fans had left. It was a cold evening and many assumed we were going to win the game, so they decided to get an early start on the hour and a half drive back to Columbus. Long story short, the second half didn't play out as we hoped. Tecumseh was able to keep us from scoring in the second half, while compiling sixteen points of their own. A field goal with less than a minute to play allowed Tecumseh to break the tie and win the game 16-13. Losing the way we did was beyond devastating. We let a game slip from under us because we took our focus away from the task at hand. The disappointing loss that ended our season turned out to be the beginning of a downward spiral.

* * *

In May 2001, six months prior to the end of my senior football season in high school, I was headed to a summer football camp, when I noticed a state highway patrol officer traveling on the other side of the highway. I glanced down at my speedometer like most people do when they spot a cop while driving. I was going a little faster than the posted speed limit of 65 mph but considering there was a Greyhound bus traveling right next to me at relatively the same speed, I felt comfortable with how fast I was going.

That comfort sort of ended when, through my rear-view mirror, I saw the patrol officer cross the grassy median, whip a u-turn, and turn on his lights. In hoping the officer wasn't coming for me, I passed the Greyhound bus and got over to the right lane, making way for the officer to pass. The next thing I knew, the officer and his red and blue flashing lights were right on my tail. I was nervous as heck. It was my first time getting pulled over by the cops. I almost got pulled over one time before, at age thirteen, when I snuck and drove my grandmother's car around the block. The police followed me, but they didn't pull me over, as I turned in an alley and they kept going. This time I wasn't so lucky. The officer gave me a ticket, claiming I was traveling at 82 mph. I begged and pleaded with the officer, trying to convince him I was not going that fast. I had no chance in convincing a reversal. He told me to fight it in court.

Throughout the summer and into the fall, I waited for a letter in the mail regarding my speeding ticket. In the meantime, I was pulled over a second time on my way to a football scrimmage in which I was running late. It seems when you're rushing, everything goes wrong. I was driving as fast as I could. Once again, I saw the red and blue lights flash in my rearview mirror. It couldn't have come at a worse time. The cop came to my window and notified me I was clocked traveling at 47 mph in a 35 mph zone. I was lucky he didn't clock me a few miles earlier when I was driving closer to 60 mph. As you could imagine, I got a ticket. Under Ohio law, if a minor gets four infraction points on their license, their license gets suspended. Considering each speeding violation is equivalent to two points and I had gotten two, I had reached the threshold.

I was summoned and attended court for the second violation. Still, I had not received anything from the first violation, but I brought it to the judge's attention during my hearing. She looked up my information and could not find any other violations on record. As I went to court that day thinking my license would be revoked, I was ecstatic to walk out of the courtroom with them still intact.

Around the time football season ended, I got the letter in the mail from Marion County summoning me to court for the speeding violation I had gotten six months prior. I was in disbelief. I couldn't understand why it took their clerk of courts six months to process a speeding ticket. At that moment, I knew the only chance I had in keeping my license was to fight the ticket in court, so I prepared to do just that. My court date was set for early January 2002, so I had roughly forty days to prepare a defense and attempt to keep my license. I researched laws and even got advice from a close friend who happened to be a seasoned Highway Patrol officer.

My court date arrived. I hoped the officer who issued me the ticket would fail to show up to court, allowing the charge to be dismissed. That hope was deflated when the uniformed officer walked in. It came time to enforce plan B: defend myself. I didn't have an attorney so I had to rely on the skills I learned in a pre-law summer class through Upward Bound. The prosecuting attorney examined the officer. I followed up with a cross examination of my own. I asked, "Isn't it true, Officer, that you used a radar gun to clock the speed of my vehicle?"

"Yes," replied the officer.

"And is it true that a radar gun expands over an area, unlike a laser gun that hits a specific target?"

"Correct."

"So, it very well could have been the large Greyhound bus that was alongside of me that your radar detected, correct?"

I looked over at the judge and saw him nodding his head at my questions and statements as if he was in agreement with me. I don't quite recall exactly what happened after that. I do know I had a good feeling that I was not going to lose my license that day. I was proven wrong once again. Those presumed favorable nods by the judge meant nothing as he found me guilty and suspended my license for three months.

That day got worse. After court, my grandmother drove me to my part-time job at Wal-Mart. I pondered the entire trip, wondering how I was going to maintain my job with limited transportation. Turns out that it didn't matter. Before making it two steps past the time clock, a manager came out of a nearby office and told me they were firing me that day. I was so angry I couldn't even offer a challenge. I simply handed over my badge, vest and box cutter and headed for the exit. Obviously, I was mad because I had just lost my license and my job, but I was even more mad that my grandmother had just dropped me off, and I had to wait until she got all the way home to call her to tell her to come back and get me (cell phones were still in their infancy at that time).

That day turned out to be a pivotal moment in my adolescence. I had overcome many adverse situations in my short years, but it seemed I was facing a difficult situation which would overtake me. While I was sitting on a bench in the entrance of Wal-Mart waiting on my ride, I picked up a magazine that had used cars for sell. I had one thought in mind: when I got my license back, I would have a new set of wheels. Without a job, I figured there was only one way to get the money; through the sale of drugs. I made a decision that day to turn to the very thing I had tried my entire life to get away from—the streets.

I knew a few small time dealers around town, so I called a couple of them up to get the scoop on the whole process. I was interested in making some quick money, but I also wanted to minimize my risk. Due to the downfall of my parents, I never wanted to mess with crack or coke, so distributing pills and marijuana seemed like the best option. After a few phone calls, I had my first deal in place with some ecstasy pills. After waiting a week or so for delivery, the phone call finally came in detailing the pickup location. I had mixed emotions as I drove to the location.

I pulled up and parked near the end of the street as I was instructed. A few minutes passed, and then a gentleman approached my car from a nearby alley. I rolled down my window and he handed me a paper bag—easy as could be. I stuffed the bag under my seat and drove home, hoping not to get pulled over with drugs and a suspended license.

I got home and raced straight to my room. I opened the paper bag and took out two small plastic bags containing about fifty pills each. It was a point of no return. I unloosened the knot on the plastic bag and dumped a few of the pills on my bed, all the while contemplating on how I would get rid of them. I played with the pills for a while, then wrapped them back up and stashed them in my drawer. I went downstairs to eat, hoping to continue to establish my plan over dinner. I barely touched the food on my plate, as I was so focused on what was in my drawer upstairs. Good, bad or indifferent, I envisioned what seemed like every possible scenario.

Then a thought came to me so strong it made me sprint from the table back to my room. I hurriedly opened the paper bag once again and grabbed a few pills out to examine. Now, this was my first time dealing with ecstasy pills, but for some reason I felt like I had seen those pills before. The color, the size, the smell—it seemed familiar. I thought really hard about any possible connections. I ran to the bathroom medicine basket and pulled out an over the counter bottle of ibuprofen. I took out an ibuprofen pill and compared it to the pills I had, and dang it, I had been fooled.

I immediately called up my contact and furiously shared what I had discovered. After a few phone calls on his end, he called me back with word that I had passed "the test." The test? I don't know if the person was trying to see if

I could tell the difference between a real pill and fake pill or I was just being bamboozled, but either way I wasn't in the mood for any games. Just think if I had gone out and tried to sell those pills. I was done.

I quickly realized drugs weren't the route for me. Once again I had let negative pressures influence my decisions and I was headed down the path to becoming another statistic. Sometimes situations like this occur where you have to recalibrate yourself. I had hit a rough patch in my life, as we all do, but I wasn't going to let it define me. I had to get back to being smart and making good decisions.

I had a lot of work to do.

Chapter Seven

College Boy

"Risk more than others think is safe. Care more than others think is wise. Dream more than others think is practical. Expect more than others think is possible."

–West Point Cadet Maximer

I was two-thirds of the way through twelfth grade and I hadn't decided which college I would attend. Part was due to the fact I was waiting on a scholarship offer to play football. Unfortunately, none of the schools I was interested in offered me. All the letters I once received from interested universities dried up as the national signing day came and went. Not even Bowling Green had an offer for me. And to think, at one point in time I had them labeled as my worst case scenario. In fact, the only schools interested in providing me any financial aid were some smaller Division II schools. Not that there is anything wrong with playing sports at a Division II school, or any school for that matter, I just felt I was good enough to play Division I ball. Plus the majority of the smaller schools didn't support my academic interests.

Sidebar Despite this dilemma, I knew education was the key to success. Boring, huh? How many times have you heard that one before? What does that even mean? Is education really the key? Are there no other keys that work? What about the keys entertainers or athletes use? Some of them find decent success, right?

Now that I have your attention . . .

I'm here to testify that education is truly the key to

success (you weren't siding with me on *questioning* education, were you? I hope not). Let's face it: there are a number of people who find success that may have dropped out of high school, skipped over college, or are just less educated in general, but, add a whole bunch of zeroes to that number and you will have calculated the number of people who weren't so lucky.

Those who find their way to fame, money, or success but lack appropriate knowledge or education stand a good chance of losing what they temporarily gained. Fame comes and goes; money comes and goes; and even the pendulum of success swings back and forth. But knowledge and education can never be taken away from you, which make them far greater attributes to have than being able to shoot a basketball, sing, or catch a football.

The fear of failure has a strong presence in education. It is present at the high school level and younger, but often times it is most revealed at the college level. Thirty percent of recent high school graduates in America choose not to attend college. You can bet a portion of those decisions is credited to fear of failure.

For the other seventy percent, they must overcome another set of fears. One is which major to choose. I know many people who had a passion to pursue one thing, but chose to major in another area because they were afraid to fail. They were afraid that their desire to be a fashion designer wouldn't pay off, thinking it would be too difficult of an industry to break into. They were afraid their parents wouldn't accept them if they didn't become a doctor or lawyer. They were afraid to enter architecture school because they thought it would be too much of a challenge.

Don't be like these people. Don't be afraid to go after what your heart truly desires. Don't fear failure.

Now let's look at the other side of the college timeline, the time when the major is chosen, completed, and the only thing left is graduation. This is when reality and fear really set in. People begin to ask *What do I do? Where do I work? Where do I live? How am I going to pay these student loans?* I challenge you not to be afraid to fail in finding those answers. Don't settle for a job in your hometown when you really want to move across the country. Don't be afraid to apply your knowledge and education and have an immediate impact in your work, your personal life, and society.

Wherever you're at on the education timeline, don't be afraid to do it all over again. Some go on for a post-graduate degree, while others may want to start over and go in a totally different direction. Either way, don't be afraid to fail.

Education is the key.

* * *

After weeks of deliberating on colleges, I narrowed my focus to three options. Each option was significantly different from the others. The first option was to settle and choose one of the smaller schools in or around Ohio which displayed interest in me. In addition to possibly receiving financial aid, this option was appealing because it would have provided me a guaranteed opportunity to play football at the collegiate level.

My second option was off the cuff, as I thought to further my education at the University of Hawaii. The fact the thought was so left field only added to my eagerness. Hawaii had a strong academic program and I was drawn to their athletics. Visions of pretty girls and sunny beaches didn't have anything to do with it, but the disadvantages were a huge factor. Being so far away from home was one of them. The other was not knowing if football was an option or not. Hawaii never recruited me for athletics, so I would have had to obtain the coaches' approval to be a part of the team. Even if I made the team, receiving playing time was another task in itself.

My third option was to stay close to home and attend The Ohio State University. The opportunity was a true blessing as a full scholarship was offered with attendance. But it was safe. It was expected. And for that I had reservations. Also, the scholarship was not an athletic scholarship. Similar to Hawaii, if I wanted to play football, I had to first win over the coaching staff. With the prestigious athletic history of Ohio State, my chance of continuing to play football was a long shot.

I reached out to the coaching staff at the University of Hawaii and sent them a tape of my football highlights. I never heard back from them. I couldn't come to grips with settling with a smaller school, so by process of elimination Ohio State was my selection. It just made sense.

Making it to college was a privilege considering where I had come from and what I had experienced. To this day, I look back and realize how blessed I was to get the opportunity. Many of my neighborhood friends never made it through high school, let alone college. There was another group that did make it through high school but still chose not to go to college. I understand college is not for everyone; however, I believe some people fear college. They fear college will be too much of a challenge. They fear it will be too expensive. They fear failure. I cherished the opportunity and was willing to accept the challenge, as I knew college would provide me the chance to grow as a person, remove myself from normality, and defy those who said I wouldn't succeed. I was ready to do great things and become someone great.

The complete feeling came when the Ohio State coaching staff told me I could join the team the following season as a walk-on.

I knew playing football for Ohio State meant I was going to be a part of one of the greatest athletic programs in the country. I also knew I needed to get a lot better. I trained like crazy over the summer trying to prepare myself for the upcoming season. And then I received some of the most exciting news ever. Instead of joining the team a few weeks into the season as most walk-ons do, I got word that the coaching staff was going to invite me to summer training camp. What was most surprising about getting invited to camp is only a certain number of players can participate, one hundred and five players to be exact, and almost all are on scholarship. Freshman walk-ons, like me, are rarely invited. In fact, I happened to be the only freshman walk-on to get the nod and attend camp in 2002.

* * *

It was the first day of summer training camp. Freshmen players had to report a few days earlier than the rest of the team to become acclimated to the college system. I didn't know what to expect. I remember walking through the doors of the facility and instantly getting, "Who the hell are you?" looks from all the players and media personnel. Many of the freshmen players got accustomed to one another during the recruiting process. Since I wasn't recruited, I didn't get that luxury.

Prior to the first day of camp I met only one freshman player which was Roy Hall. Roy and I took our freshman orientation tour together. As for all the other players, with a few exceptions who had gotten a lot of publicity, they were just as new to me as I was to them. The media, on the other hand, seemed to be familiar with everyone—except me, of course. Cameras were flashing and reporters were everywhere, hopping from one player to the next, jotting down notes and voice recording conversations. It was like being on the red carpet in Hollywood. I just sat back and took it all in.

It wasn't long before a reporter came up to me for an interview. I was extremely nervous yet enthused someone cared enough to talk to me. The reporter asked me all sorts of questions ranging from how fast I was to what my expectations were. Some I was unprepared for, but I answered the best I could with confidence and humility.

After our media obligations were handled, we made our way across the street to our practice facility known as The Woody Hayes Athletic Center, or better yet, "The Woody," to complete our physicals. As I assumed our physicals would take on the traditional form of a doctor hitting your knee with a knee hammer and making you cough a few times, I didn't change into athletic gear. That was a big mistake.

As soon as we walked into the The Woody, the strength and conditioning coaches had about four or five field drills set up for us to compete in. Lacking the proper attire to compete, I had to run and find the equipment manager to ask for a pair of shoes and shorts to replace my jeans and shell toe Addidas. I was given a pair of shorts and a pair of used turf shoes. Initially, I thought the used shoes were maybe the only pair the manager could find due to the urgency. I later found out there was a separate standard when it came to equipment for walk-ons.

Nonetheless, I was able to complete my drills. One

drill in particular, the short shuttle, really set the tone for me. I completed the drill just under four seconds, which happened to be the fastest of anyone else. As I walked back to the end of the line, I recall the looks on some being just as they were earlier: "Who the hell are you?"

After a few days of practice, the upper classmen arrived and we had our first team meeting as a whole and the freshmen players got introduced to a couple of traditions our head coach, Jim Tressel, had established. One was the entire freshman class learning and singing the OSU Fight Song, "Across the Field," to the rest of the team. The tradition goes, the freshmen have to sing the song to the team every night until the quality is liked and approved by the upper classmen. Generally, the upper classmen give the freshman a hard time by not approving the song for a week or two or three, while booing every other attempt in the meantime.

Another tradition included the daily reading of "The Winner's Manual," which was a compilation of various material including articles, poems, and quotes associated with certain characteristics such as respect, discipline, humility, etc. Every morning we would spend a few minutes reading through the material. At the close of our first team meeting, Coach Tressel requested everyone turn to a specific page and follow along as he recited the passage: "Every morning in Africa, a gazelle wakes up. It knows it must run faster than the fastest lion or it will be killed. Every morning the lion wakes up. It knows is must outrun the slowest gazelle or it will starve to death. It doesn't matter whether you are a lion or a gazelle, when the sun comes up, you'd better be running."

Gasps and sighs were heard all across the room after the reading. I was confused at first, but was quickly informed he was referencing our early morning conditioning test the following day. When I learned *twenty* half gassers were on the books as our conditioning test—one half gasser was equal to sprinting across the width of the football field and back—I realized the gasps and sighs were completely in order.

A week or so into camp I got hold of the article written by the reporter who interviewed me on the first day. I was excited to see what my first article at OSU detailed. I read it once. Then again. Then a third time. Imbedded in the article were quotes such as, "Smith has neither the size . . . nor speed . . . to immediately impress anyone," and, "The freshman cornerback showed up . . . carrying an army duffel bag that made him look more like a member of ROTC than OSU football." I was thrown yet fueled by the reporter's comments and opinions. Although criticism like this was nothing new to me, I did not expect or appreciate the shade. I was once again determined to prove success to those who anticipated my failure.

The 2002 football season got underway and we were on a roll. Classes began after the first few weeks and although it helped diversify my stringent schedule, balancing football, academics, and social life was challenging. There was football practice, football games, football film study, classes, homework, parties, and then more football. But we were winning so there was no complaining. By the end of the season we were undefeated, crowned Big Ten Champions and headed to the National Championship game. Unfortunately, that same success did not carry over into my studies. I struggled through a couple of courses and ended up with the worse grade point average I had ever earned.

We were 13-0 and headed to Tempe, Arizona for the National Championship game against the University of

Miami. The Hurricanes had been crowned champions the year prior so it was natural for us to be considered underdogs—not to mention almost half of our wins that season were decided by seven points or less. Nevertheless, we were optimistic and confident in our ability to be champions. A couple of players returned for their senior season specifically to win it all. Being National Champions was a goal we set for ourselves before the season and we put forth every effort to achieve it.

A team meeting was called following one of our last practices in Columbus before we headed to Arizona. The purpose of the meeting was to go over final details about the trip, travel arrangements and so forth. It also detailed the final count of players who would make the trip. Just as in camp, there was a cutoff limit for the number of players which could travel. This limit happened to be one hundred. Well, we had one hundred and five players in camp and added more walk-ons once the season started, so simple math puts us well over one hundred. Our director of operations informed us the final list of names was located in the locker room. I grew nervousness and after the meeting went to check the list. As I scanned the list up and down, it reminded me of not making the cut for the basketball team in ninth grade. After a thorough check, it was official: I was among the twenty or so players who weren't going to Arizona with the team.

I was mad. Furious. Not to say that I was better than anyone else, but it was a big coincidence that I was on the same list as all the other freshman walk-ons who hadn't quite put in the work I had, as they didn't join the team until well after the season started. I had worked hard throughout the summer and the season to share the same experiences as my counterparts who were on scholarship—at least I thought so.

I was not alone on that thought. After making my way back to my dorm room, I got a call from Coach Dantonio, the coach who essentially paved the way for me to join the team and participate in camp. He shared his disappointment of me not being apart of the travel team and assured me he would attempt to change it. He did just that. There was one stipulation though; in order to actually make a contribution to the team and not just take up a spot, I had to agree to play as a wide receiver on the offensive scout team. Although I normally played defense, I didn't mind one bit. I would've washed jock straps to make that trip. Okay, maybe not jock straps, but you get my drift.

We arrived in Arizona the day after Christmas for what turned out to be one of the most memorable weeks of my life. From the moment we stepped off the plane, we were treated like royalty. Escorts guided us to our luxurious resort where the hospitality was second to none. Food, game, activities—anything we wanted was at our fingertips. We had to keep in mind that we were not on vacation but on more of a business trip.

Game day arrived and it was time to take care of that business. The energy of the players and coaches took on the form of a quiet, focused, ready-to-attack type of energy. The meeting rooms were quiet. The hallways were quiet. Our pre-game meal was eaten in silence. The only noise in the dinning hall came from the ting of the silverware against the china. That is, until our four captains got up to share a few words. The excitement in the room grew after each one spoke. The last captain got so worked up that he excitedly flipped over a table full of food. Unfair as it may have been for the hotel staff, a cheer erupted from the rest of the team. It was time to play.

A tense battle took place on the football field on the evening of January 3, 2003. The air was warm, the skies were clear, and it was a perfect evening for a football. Although I knew I wasn't playing in the game, mentally, I was on the field every play. Both teams exchanged hard-hitting tackles, touchdowns, and turnovers. One of the most pivotal plays in the game resulted in two turnovers on one play. Our quarterback threw an interception in our end zone, and as the defender ran the opposite direction with the ball, Maurice Clarett, our running back, chased him down, stripped the ball, and recovered it.

After having a lead for most of the second half, Miami managed to tie the game at the end of regulation with a field goal. Forced into overtime, the Hurricanes got the ball first and scored a touchdown. As we attempted to answer with a score of our own, we came up short with an incomplete pass on fourth down. Simultaneously, fireworks were set off and the Hurricanes and their fans began to rush the field. My body instantly went numb. I was revived however, learning the game was not over due to a flag being thrown on the play. A defensive penalty was called which extended our chance to score. We ended up scoring forcing the game to double overtime, scored again in the second overtime, and stopped Miami at their 1 yard line to secure a victory over the Hurricanes and accomplishing our goal of becoming National Champions.

Being on the sideline in uniform with my team during that victory is an experience I will never forget. It was an ultimate victory for OSU as well as myself. It was proof that underdogs can and will prevail.

Chapter Eight
MORE LESSONS LEARNED

"The best thing you can give someone is a chance."

–Anonymous

After winning the National Championship, all was well in the world of football. It couldn't get much better. Yet there were some areas outside of football which needed my attention. One area was in the academic department. My grades had improved from my rocky first quarter start, but I wasn't sure if I had chosen the right field to study, which was mechanical engineering. The decision didn't have much rhyme or reason outside of a conversation with my high school counselor which uncovered my strong interest in areas dealing with math and sciences. As my first few quarters of college revealed the relatively challenging subject matter of engineering, I worried I wouldn't be able to dedicate enough time to studying and learning the material due to football. I spent a few weeks exploring other majors and talking through my decision with friends. Ultimately, my decision was to finish what I started. I knew whichever major I chose to study would be challenging to some degree and I decided to accept my challenge versus run from it.

I have often noticed when the going gets tough, people tend to look for an easy way out. The sense of failure kicks in. Situations like this often separate those who desire to be great from those who are fine with being average. I was once told, "If it was easy, everyone would do it."

My second year classes were slightly easier than my first. I'm not sure if the material got easier, the professors explained it better, or I just had better focus. That was until I ran into one math class which almost got the best of me. Prior to the class, I always considered math as my strong suit. However, the professor that particular quarter seemed not to be teaching math but German or something. Not that I could not understand his words, but I couldn't follow his teachings. The proofs and theorems were not sticking at all. After our first midterm, I knew I was in a dilemma. I had bombed the test, and at the rate I was going it seemed almost impossible to bounce back.

I scheduled a meeting with the professor to see how I could improve my grades and give myself a chance to pass the class. The professor gave me two options. Option One was to drop the class. Normally, it wouldn't have been a bad idea. The problem was if I had dropped the class it would have affected my credit hours and my status as a full-time student, hence affecting my eligibility for football. I explained I could not by any means drop the class. So he offered Option Two. I hoped he would extend an invitation for extra credit or provide some sort of leeway. Instead, the offer was for me to continue with the class solely to get a glimpse of the remaining material so that I could be better prepared when I retook the class. I was offended when the professor presented this option. It was like he had absolutely no confidence I would pass the class.

Knowing I couldn't drop the class, I set out once again to prove I would overcome and succeed. I studied like a mad man. I hooked up with others in the class who actually understood the material for study sessions. After a lot of hard work, a couple more midterms, and a final test, I not only elevated my grade to passing, but I got a B+.

My personal relationships with family and friends also needed attention and improvement. Having a correct balance in life is very important. At times I would get so consumed with school and football that I didn't have time to spend with those who mattered most. To this day I feel I missed opportunities with loved ones, especially my siblings, because of my limited availability. The relationships between my siblings and I were already disadvantaged because we did not grow up in the same household. Being the oldest by seven years didn't help much either. I was more of an enforcer of rules rather than a partner in crime. I had a responsibility as a role model to show both my sisters, who also grew up without a father figure, as well as my brother that you can do great things if you put your mind to it.

I also needed to restore the relationship between my grandmother and myself. As I mentioned before, throughout my teenage years my grandmother and I didn't quite see eye to eye. Going off to college was a relief, but my absence only acted as a bandage for some problems, leaving major issues still unresolved. And let me tell you, my grandmother is definitely one to hold onto a grudge. I decided to move back home after my freshman year of college to save money and help reestablish the great relationship we once had. I had to understand I was dealing with an older, stubborn, egotistic woman who only really wanted the best for me; she had to understand that I wasn't five years old anymore and as a young man there were decisions I needed to make without her input.

One of those decisions pertained to an appropriate time to come home at night. My grandmother gave as much ground as she was going to give when she stated 2 a.m. was a sufficient time. It was like high school all over again. As a college student, 2 a.m. would never work. Most parties don't even end until 2:30 a.m., not to mention after parties. I had to respectfully convey my stance on no curfew. I had just spent an entire year doing as I wished, coming and going as I pleased. There was no going back. I assured my grandmother I would be conscious of her feelings and use discretion when I went out, but there would be no curfew.

A lot changed during my transition from freshman to sophomore in my academics and social life, and football followed suit. Following one of my training sessions at the end of my first year, I was pulled aside by Coach Dantonio. He said I really needed to work hard throughout the summer and prove that I should be invited back to camp, as there were no guarantees for the upcoming season. I was thrown off by the information, but I gave my word I would do my best. I respected Coach Dantonio because he was always a straight shooter and I liked that. At times his demeanor could be intimidating, as he was one to have a smile one instance which would quickly morph into a grimace the next. I knew I had some work to do to once again prove myself. Pulling from the conversation I had with Coach Dantonio, I coined and began to work from the slogan, "I'm going to do what I can do. If I can do it, I'm going to do it."

The slogan and my hard work paid off when I was invited back to camp my second year. I was excited and relieved to maintain my position on the team, but I was no longer content with just being a body. Neither were my coaches. During a meeting with my position coach, I was challenged to elevate my play so that I would be a part of the weekly travel team. The way it was spelled out for me was if I wasn't on the bus with the travel team by season's end, I would run the risk of being cut the following year. So what did I do? I coined another phrase: "Cut the Bus." I hung signs of the phrase all over my locker and even had a necklace made with the letters CTB. Needless to say, I made the travel team.

Our first away game during the 2003 season was against the Wisconsin Badgers at Camp Randall Stadium. We were undefeated on the season and I hadn't experienced a loss since I began my collegiate career. It was a night game—and it was crazy. We went through our pre-game warm-ups as usual. Everything was fine. But after we came back out from the locker room to start the game, it was raining and the temperature felt like it dropped 20 degrees. I knew it was going to be a long evening. I realized why critics claim Camp Randall is a tough place to play. The Wisconsin fans were throwing paper and bottles at us on the sidelines and chanting, "Suck dick, eat shit, suck dick, eat shit!" most of the game. At one point, they even had a streaker run across the field. Although the streaker was entertaining, it was of no comparison to witnessing the entire stadium jumping around at the start of the fourth quarter to the 1990's musical hit, "Jump Around."

We lost. My first traveling experience was a nightmare. The somberness in the locker room would have made you think we were at a funeral. I didn't know how to act. What was protocol after a loss? Was I allowed to speak? It was my first rodeo. I followed suit and remained quiet like everyone else.

As it does with most things, time healed our loss against the Badgers; the Michigan Wolverines, better know to us as That Team Up North, handed us our only other loss during the 2003 season. It was unfortunate we suffered that loss because if we had won we were projected to go back to the National Championship game.

Each year, the week leading up to the Michigan game was always special. Former players and coaches tend to visit the team that week and share what a privilege it is to be apart of the great rivalry. That year was no different.

The coaches were intense; the players were excited. I was thrilled because it was to be my first time traveling to the "Big House." I was also excited to see some of my family who lived in Michigan, which I had promised tickets to the game.

The day before we were set to travel to Michigan, I got a phone call from my position coach. He told me to be at practice a few minutes earlier because he needed to talk with me. I didn't quite know what to expect, but I knew it didn't sound like good news. I arrived at his office just as he requested. He sat me down and delivered what at the time seemed liked the ultimate blow. He informed me that I would not be traveling to Michigan for the game. I was heated. I pleaded my case hoping for a sympathetic reversal but it got me nowhere. I was most devastated about the fact that I had to call my family in Michigan and tell them I was not traveling to the game. They were the only people I told. I kept it from everyone else because I was embarrassed and ashamed. I didn't even tell my girlfriend. I played as if I was at the game, making sure not to be seen or heard from until the team was expected to return to Columbus. In actuality I watched the disappointing loss on television with a teammate who also didn't travel.

* * *

As the saying goes, "There is a time and place for everything." My decision to move back home during college served its purpose, but after a year and a half it was no longer the place I wanted to be and it was time for me to move out. This decision saddened my grandmother but her ego didn't let her show it one bit. Her tough-as-nails personality displayed an eagerness for me to go but I knew she would miss having me around, even if it was just to have someone to yell at.

For months I saved up every little bit of money I could in anticipation of moving. In addition to my quarterly financial aid refund checks, I worked at a nearby warehouse during the off season which sold and restored valves. It was light work and I enjoyed working there, so I managed to pick up extra hours, most of which were spent clowning around with the guys and eating Subway. The facility actually had a nice café area, but the guys I usually ate with chose to eat in the dust and dirt. They were rough around the edges and didn't care to be in the clean café where the television continually played soap operas.

After a few good months of work, I had managed to save a decent amount of money. At that point, I had one goal in mind: to move out as soon as possible. That's when I found out apartment hunting was a much tougher and lengthier process than I imagined. Although it was my very first apartment, I had a set of standards to be met, one of the most important being price. Weeks went by until I finally came across an apartment which suited my needs. After talking with the property manager, I identified a target date to move in. I was excited about my move and began preparing.

Then I got a call from one of my good friends. It just so happened I was planning to move right around the time of spring break. A number of my friends were planning to go to Cancun for vacation and asked if I wanted to join them. My first thought was of course. I had yet to experience a college spring break and I looked forward to witnessing moments similar to what is seen on television and the popular DVD series, "Girls Gone Wild." My previous spring breaks had been fairly boring, as I would stay in Columbus and work on football drills at my old high school, trying to get myself prepared for spring practices. However, going on vacation would have set my move back by a couple months. I had a decision to make. After brief consideration, the goal to move out as soon as possible won.

I had locked down my apartment and move-in date so it was time to buy the furnishings, another process which wasn't as easy as I thought. From color to fabric to size and then of course price, shopping was nuts. I didn't need to have everything, but there were a few must have items and they needed to be nice. The first was a decent sized television. I mean, what guy doesn't want a big TV to watch sports or play video games? The second was a nice couch. I figured since I would be spending a lot of time watching my nice television, I needed a comfy place to sit. Plus, for entertaining purposes, I wanted guests to have respectable, clean seating. Lastly, but probably most important, I wanted a big bed. I was fortunate in having the luxury of a queen-sized bed for most of my years, but it was time for an upgrade. After my games, or a long day of school and practice, I wanted to be able to stretch all the way out on a king-sized bed.

I visited a few stores and closely watched the days those stores had items on sale. I was able to settle on a nice couch and television fairly easy. The bed presented a greater challenge, one of the reasons being king-sized beds aren't cheap. But I was not willing to compromise on size. I searched and searched from one store to another, flopping on and off an assortment of beds to get a feel for what I liked. Upon finding one to my liking, I would then flip over the price tag, which signaled I needed to keep looking.

My bed searching began to become somewhat of a hassle. Approaching the point of frustration, I found my way to a discount mattress store, convinced I would find what I was looking for. I walked in the doors, went straight to the center of the store, and spotted a king-sized bed I was ready to make mine. The mattress wasn't as thick as some of the others I had seen. It wasn't as sturdy either. But it was a king, and the price was right. The store assistant helping me said I could get the frame, mattress and box springs for $600. He also mentioned they had a "six months same as cash" payment plan. It was a no-brainer; I would get the bed, pay it off in six months and all would be good. The assistant proceeded to fill out the paperwork to get the financing process going. I was told it would take a day or two to get authorized, and I could come back then to get the bed. I went home feeling good knowing I finally had the big items I wanted.

A couple days passed and I got a call from the mattress store. My excitement faded as I was informed the financing was denied. I couldn't understand why. I felt I had pretty decent credit and the amount was only $600. It wasn't like it was a car or anything. Highly upset from the phone call, I gathered myself and thought of a second option, which was to simply have my grandmother co-sign on the financing.

I told my grandmother the predicament I was in and I asked her to co-sign for the financing for my bed. I ensured her I would take care of the payments and she would have no worries or responsibility. After a long drawn out story, one which I heard numerous times, about how she co-signed on a loan for my mother many years prior and ended up having to pay the balance, she said no. She said no! I was pissed. Here I was trying to move out and cross the next bridge of my life and I couldn't get even a little help from my own grandmother. To this day, I don't know if her decision was intended to disrupt my move or if her reasoning was genuine.

By now, my frustration turned to pure anger. For most of my life I felt like I had to figure out things on my own. I had grown accustom to making a way for myself and this situation was panning out to be no different. I did, however, have one last option for help. As a last resort, I figured I could turn to my mother and ask for her help. I knew she didn't have an 800 credit score, but again, with the loan being minimal, I didn't foresee an issue. My mother agreed to be the co-signer, so we went back to the store and reapplied for financing. We had to of course wait another couple days. I am not really superstitious but I felt strongly about my third attempt. Days later I got a phone call from the mattress store. I was a bit nervous, but confident we were all set.

The financing was denied once more. By that time I knew it wasn't meant to be.

Throughout the entire search, I prayed and asked God to help me. I questioned Him, asking why there were so many obstacles and roadblocks. Then, knowing I was unsuccessful at everything I tried, I just turned it over to Him. I had the faith that God would work it out. I didn't know when or how, but I knew He would do it. Not more than a week or so went by when I was talking about my situation with an acquaintance. I was then directed to contact a specific person at the same store I had been so unsuccessful with. After a brief phone conversation, I was presented with the opportunity to purchase a mattress that was ten times better than the one I originally wanted for less than $600. It was a dream come true. God proved to me once again that no matter how hard we try to get things done, sometimes we just need to let Him handle it.

Chapter Nine

POLITICS & SACRIFICE

"A man's doubts and fears are his worst enemies."

–William Wrigley Jr.

It was that time of the year again: camp. I was heading into my fourth year and had come a long way from my first camp as a freshman, but still hadn't quite reached the pinnacle. Over the years, I slowly gained the respect and trust from the coaching staff and made my way to the playing field through special teams. In comparing my situation to the typical walk-on, I had overachieved, as most receive only limited playing time. But comparing what I had achieved versus what I wanted to achieve, I still had a long way to go.

Sometimes the opportunities a player gets does not stem from their abilities but their perceived potential. The potential of a walk-on is often overlooked. Although I felt as if my talents were just as good as others ahead of me, I had to deal with being overlooked in many situations. It got to the point where, in my mind, my talents went from being overlooked to merely disregarded. Yes, even collegiate football can be political.

Throughout the first week in camp during my fourth year, in addition to special teams, I had been practicing with the second and third defensive units as a safety. The two starting safety spots were pretty much locked up by the players who had started those positions the two seasons prior, so the coaches were looking for solid backups. I was in the hunt. Not only was I in competition with all the other safeties but in direct competition with my camp roommate.

Being that we were both walk-ons, we were eagerly vying for the spot with the second unit. I was practicing hard. My efforts were not only observed by the coaches, but the front office personnel as well. I even received several "Good job" and "Way to compete" comments after a few practices. I felt like I had a chance.

During our second week of camp, our safeties coach said they were shuffling players around and posted a revised depth chart. My name was not listed with the second or third unit; I had dropped all the way down to practicing with the fourth team. To add insult to injury, the players ahead of me were younger. One was even a freshman. To be clear, the freshman had not shown a greater talent, nor did he know after a week as much as I knew as a fourth year player. It was a prime example of the politics which players like me faced.

That particular day, politics or no politics, I wasn't having it. How dare I be treated like this? I took the practice field in rage, so much so that after participating on special teams in the first half of practice, I decided to sideline myself the rest of the day. I figured if my efforts on defense weren't appreciated, I wasn't going to give any effort at all. I ignored my position coach and remained on one knee as he waived the fourth team defense onto the practice field. I told the other safeties to stay in and take all my reps. I didn't get better that day as a player, but I sure felt better after my solo boycott. The funny thing is, I don't know if my coach even noticed.

The following week or so of camp didn't prove to be much better. As I mentioned, my camp roommate and I were both walk-ons. During the evenings when we weren't battling each other, we frequently shared our thoughts and personal goals for the team. We both had a couple things in common. Outside of the safety position we sought, we both hoped to receive an athletic scholarship that year during camp. Despite my rants of being overlooked, Coach Tressel did make an attempt to reward deserving walk-ons by placing them on athletic scholarship. It didn't necessarily mean you would receive more playing time, but it did even the playing field somewhat.

During the remaining week or so of camp, there was a lot of talk about which walk-ons would be offered scholarships. There were a number of senior walk-ons who had paid their dues; however, there was only one other walk-on who was expected to play more than I was in the upcoming season. Considering the scholarships were to be earned rather than just given out, there was no doubt in my mind that I was on the ballot.

During a team meeting, Coach Tressel announced there were a handful of walk-on players to be placed on scholarship. He rattled off the names and if you have followed the storyline up until this point, you can guess I wasn't one of them. It wasn't as if I needed the scholarship for financial reasons as some players did, because my tuition was already covered. It was more of a respect thing for me. It was another disappointment.

The unfortunate series of events throughout camp led me to question my attitude and commitment to the team. Although I never acted out or said much, I was fed up with the roller coaster ride which had been my entire football career. The season started and I still hadn't made my way back to the second defensive unit. I was playing a lot on special teams though, so I couldn't complain too much. I just stayed quiet and did my job. Then one evening, a teammate and I began comparing our college football experiences. He happened to be a walk-on. As you can see, we kind of stick together. We shared our unique stories from beginning to end with a lot of mixed feelings and emotions.

That conversation led me, for the first time, to truly consider finishing that year and foregoing my last season. Normally when you hear about a college player foregoing their last season, it is to enter into the professional side of sports. That wasn't the case for me. I thought I'd spend my last year concentrating solely on academics, as my engineering classes were requiring more and more time for studying. The bottom line was that I felt I was at the top of a glass ceiling. I could see there were more opportunities but felt I would never have the chance to reach them.

All the while, I could hear my grandmother's voice in my head. On several occasions she suggested I relinquish my football duties and strictly focus on schooling. Even with my frustrations, not once did I ever let her suggestions penetrate my mind. I would simply tell her she didn't understand. But maybe she did understand. Maybe she knew long before I did that I would eventually come to a crossroads where I had to make a decision to keep going straight or turn in a different direction. In the days following that conversation, I thought long and hard about what I wanted to do and what was best for me. After talking it over with one of my closest friends, I came to a conclusion which affected the rest of my life.

There is a difference between quitting and being a quitter. One can lead to a life of turmoil and a stockpile of unfinished business, while the other can lead to clarity and success. I am no quitter. I'll go to the depths to explore every possible solution before I walk away from something. The question which lingered in my thoughts of walking away from football was had I truly done everything possible? The answer was no. Shortly after discovering I hadn't explored every possibility, I made a commitment to stay with the team throughout my last season, no matter how many low points I still had left on the roller coaster. I also vowed I would go all out, leaving behind no regrets or shoulda-coulda-woulda's.

I knew my one hundred and ten percent effort alone would still only get me so far. I needed an outside source to help me breakthrough the glass ceiling and reach the next level. The only one I knew who could provide such assistance was God. He proved time and time again that He could handle things that I couldn't. I prayed and offered up to Him my entire situation so that He would have total control from the top down. Even though I know no prayer request is too big for God, I still felt as if I was asking for a lot. I felt since I was asking God to pour out all these blessings on me, there had to be something I could do to show I was worthy—something I could sacrifice.

In ancient times, people would use animals as sacrificial offerings. I didn't have any animals, plus nowadays with PETA, that wouldn't fly. I had to come up with something, but what? I was a pretty good guy. What could I give up? What could I sacrifice worthy enough for God? Not being able to think of anything on my own, I prayed and asked God what I could do to prove to Him that I was sincere about my request.

I got an answer almost immediately.

I was caught off guard by the speediness of the response and the response itself. I was almost certain I had misheard God's response in what He wanted me to do. There was no way it could be done. Well, there was a way; I just needed a lot of time to figure out how. A lot of time.

Days went by, then weeks, and I still had not acted on what God suggested I do. Honestly, I wasn't ready. I spent the entire time trying to come up with a second comparable sacrifice to serve as a replacement. I thought about it everyday. It may have just been my conscience, but I also started to notice subtle signs that reminded me of what God wanted me to do. I still wasn't ready.

The regular season had come to a close and we were once again headed to Arizona for a bowl game. Arizona had become like a home away from home, as we had been invited four out of my five years to play there. I had grown accustom to the four hour plane ride from Columbus to Phoenix. However, the plane ride I experienced my fourth year was a different experience than I was used to. Very little talking came from my seat. It was like I was in a daze the entire plane ride. As we cruised the blue sky, I could only think about one thing, the same thing I had been thinking about for weeks on end: the sacrifice God had set on my heart.

It was frustrating not being able to shake the thoughts out of my mind. Even when I tried not to think about it, everything I did, saw or heard ended up somehow linking back to it. Those once subtle signs had become not so subtle anymore. It was like the inevitable was going to take place whether I was ready or not.

Once we arrived in Arizona, one of the first things I did was hook up with a close friend and former teammate of mine who also made the trip down from Ohio. We grabbed a bite to eat and had a good time reliving some old memories. He came from a religious background and I thought it was the perfect opportunity to reveal a snippet of what I was going through to maybe get some advice. Initially, I didn't disclose all the details and purposely failed to mention the sacrifice I had been contemplating for several weeks. That was until my friend shared with me that he had been making some changes in his life to better align himself with his beliefs. One of the biggest changes he was attempting was to refrain from having premarital sex. At that moment, it was like I received the ultimate sign from God. How ironic was it that the change my friend was attempting was the exact response I had received from God weeks back. The sacrifice God placed on my heart was to abstain from having premarital sex. In talking with my friend and finally disclosing all the details, I was convinced that I had to stop having sex.

The issue was no longer what I needed to do, but when I needed to do it. Should I wait to get back to Ohio? Do I talk it over with my girlfriend first? Do I get it in one last time? I needed to know. I had been sexually active since high school and I couldn't imagine how my life would function without it, hence the reason why I was so skeptical about the sacrifice in the first place. I spent the next few days pondering what would be the most optimal time to implement such a drastic change in my life. I couldn't quite decide. Then one evening it all made sense.

It was New Year's Eve. We had been in Arizona for about four or five days. The first few days we had an extended curfew and were able to go out at night. The curfew shortened as we got closer to game day. Two days out from the game, our curfew was 10 p.m. That meant if we wanted to take part in any New Year's Eve celebrations, we had to do it from our room. That was okay by me. I wasn't used to bringing in the New Year at a party or club anyhow. I usually brought it in at church. Although I wasn't at church then, I decided I would bring in the New Year by praying and reading a couple scriptures in my room by myself. It was fitting considering all the stuff I had recently been dealing with.

10 p.m. arrived. In the winter months Arizona is two hours behind Ohio, so I started getting all the "Happy New

Year" calls and messages. Once that started, I figured there was no point on waiting until midnight Pacific Standard Time. I took out the courtesy Bible from the night table stand. With the idea of refraining from sex heavy on my mind, I thought I should find a scripture which dealt in that area. I looked through the concordance to find an appropriate scripture, and landed on the key term: temptation. Since sex has a lot to do with temptation, I decided to take a closer look at one of the scriptures it highlighted. I flipped to the page of James 1:12 and began reading. Seven words into the verse I felt a sensation come over me which I had never felt before. I could not fight it any longer. Instantly, I broke down and began to cry as I read the words, "Blessed is the man that endureth temptation." It all made perfect sense. The full scripture reads, "Blessed is the man that endureth temptation: for when he is tried, he shall receive the crown of life which the Lord hath promised to them that love him."

This was one of the most profound moments in my life. I could only think of one person who would understand what was happening in my life. I called my mother. As I mentioned earlier, my mother had made a 180-degree turn from her previous habits of abusing drugs and alcohol. At that time she had been clean for about six years. During those six years she committed herself to being a Christian and was even ordained as a minister. Due to it being New Year's Eve, my mother was still up and answered my call. I told her everything. She listened carefully and then comforted me with an ideology which provided me with even more clarity. Her ideology was this:

God has set forth a designated and unique path that He wants each of us to be on. That path is filled with blessings and ultimately leads to an everlasting life with Him.

What happens is, through sin and being disobedient, people usually get off the path God has set and take a detoured route. Even on the detoured route, God still blesses us because He loves us. Even thieves, murderers and rapists are blessed in some way, shape, or form. Yet those blessings don't even remotely compare to what God really wants to give to us.

All of us at some point experience the detoured road. Unfortunately, some never realize the road they're on is a detour. Others recognize they are not heading down the path God has set but hesitate to make the necessary changes to get on it. Then there are those who understand they are on a detoured path and want to connect to the right path as soon as possible. The difference between the latter two is the amount of blessings missed by delaying getting on the right path. Every day, every hour, every minute we spend away from God's path, we are missing out on blessings. Once you've missed them, you've missed them. There is no going back to get them. You will never know if you missed the blessing which could have changed your entire life while you were busy on the detoured path.

After hearing that, it was evident that I needed to act immediately. I could not wait to get back to Ohio or talk to my girlfriend or get it in one last time. After talking with my mother, I got down on my knees and made a commitment to God right then that I would refrain from having sex until I was married. I wanted God to help me become the best athlete I could be; He wanted me to quit having sex. I had the faith that if I kept up my end of the bargain, more blessings would come my way than I could ever imagine.

It didn't take long for me to reap the benefits of my commitment. Within two days, my commitment transpired into a blessing which could have only come from God. After our bowl game, two of our starting defensive backs decided to skip their senior season and declared to enter the NFL. The other two starting defensive backs were already seniors and were graduating, leaving four vacant starting positions to be filled. I knew two of the four were pretty much taken, but two were wide open. God opened a door for me which no man could have opened.

That open door truly changed my entire life. It started with football, but quickly trickled down to the relationships I had with others, including my girlfriend. It definitely took some getting used to on both ends, but unquestionably, not having sex allowed the bond between my girlfriend and I to become stronger and we were able to strengthen our commitment and love towards one another.

Eventually, I was able to see the big picture and realized that success in football and with my personal relationships were only a small piece of the pie. It became clear that the purpose of my commitment was much deeper than me benefiting from becoming a better football player or boyfriend. It was to become a better child of God. I was determined more than ever to try to walk in the way that God wanted me to walk. Notice I said try because, I nor anyone else will never truly get it all the way right, but as long as we are trying, we're at least heading in the right direction.

Sidebar

Speaking of heading in the right direction, in regards to religion, what have you done lately? I ask what have you done lately because that's the world we live in, right? In school our grades are not determined on how we performed last semester. At our jobs our boss could care less about the project we worked on several years ago.

Spouses are not interested about past efforts. Our evaluation comes from the notion of what have we done *lately*. That same notion should apply to our religious beliefs. It is not enough to honor God a few times a year and think we're in good standing. It is not enough to stay spiritually stagnant as believers. It is not enough to hold onto our God and His words but not share the Gospel with others. Just as our teachers, bosses, and spouses want to know, God also wants to know, *what have you done lately?*

Often times in life, in order to move forward and take the next step, we make some sort of commitment. For example, when we go from being unemployed to employed, we make a commitment to the employer that we are going to show up for work. Or when we go from being single to married, we make a commitment to our partner to always love and be faithful. So why is it in our religion, when we claim we want to move forward and grow closer to God, we are hesitant to make a commitment? It is because of our fear of failure. The last thing we want to do is fail in honoring our commitment to God.

If we don't uphold our commitment at work, we get fired, but we can find another job. If we don't uphold our commitment to our spouse, we get a divorce, but we can find another partner. But if we don't uphold our commitment to God, the world is going to come crashing down on us—at least that's what we think.

The truth of the matter is that God wants us to commit to Him. He does want us to also honor our commitments, but know that He is not going to fire us nor leave us in the event we fall short. God is a forgiving God; He is a loving God. Best of all, all He wants from us is to show an increased effort toward Him. A failed attempt of commitment is better than no attempt at all.

I challenge you to trust God, have faith in Him, and don't let the fear of failure keep you from all the blessings He has in store for you.

Chapter Ten
Two Ships Emerge

"...Those who work the hardest, who subject themselves to the strictest discipline, who give up certain pleasurable things in order to achieve a goal, are the happiest..."

–Brutus Hamilton

When someone asks, "How's it going?" I generally reply, "I can't complain." I follow up with, "Well, I could, but I'm sure you don't want to hear that." In the spring prior to my senior year, I truly didn't have much to complain about. For the first time I felt I had a genuine opportunity to prove myself on the football field. I was committed to go over and beyond whatever asked and I knew with the help of God I would have a darn good shot at realizing my dreams.

Just when I thought things couldn't get any better, they did. Every year, Coach Tressel requested each player to fill out a goal sheet. The goal sheet included short and long-term goals covering an array of areas including football, religion, family, etc. He then would meet with every player, review their goal sheets and talk through strategies to help them reach their goals. There were two distinct goals I had on my sheet for my senior year. One was to get an athletic scholarship, which had been consistent with my last few goal sheets. The other goal was to be included in the latest edition of college football video games being created that year. I failed to be recognized on the games in the years prior.

Upon my review with Coach Tressel, he eluded one of the goals would be completed by the end of our meeting and the other we would still have to work towards. He pulled out a document which was an official offering for an athletic scholarship and asked me to sign. I felt it was long overdue, but it couldn't have come at a better time. It was an exciting moment. Receiving the athletic scholarship didn't have a major impact on my financial situation, but it did in other areas. It meant I finally got two sets of equipment like the rest of the scholarship players. It meant I got to eat delicious waffles on Friday morning at the training table. And it meant I finally gained the trust and respect from the coaches which I had so longed for.

Spring practices began. It was my time to shine. In addition to the scholarship, I was finally given the chance to practice with the first team defense. My position coach, Tim Beckman, believed in me and felt through all my hard work and perseverance that I earned a chance to prove myself. To this day, I am forever grateful of him in giving me that chance. With that said, spring practices are designed for competition, so practicing with the first team in the spring does not automatically equate to being a starter once the season begins. I was aware of that and so was everyone else, including the media. I often read articles and blogs of how I was likely to be beat out by the other players I was competing against. I learned to never get too high or too low with the media. I just blocked it out, stayed true, and focused on the task at hand.

Spring practices ended and I finished where I had started with the first team defense. Competition was stiff but I never let up off the throttle. As we moved into the summer months, I had no plans on easing up. In summer's past I had worked, but I had a different plan that summer. Instead of working, I wanted to dedicate my time to extra practice and film study. There were to be no excuses why I wasn't starting in the first game of the season. But there was one problem: since I didn't want to work, I had to figure out how I would pay my rent and other expenses.

There was only one person I could turn to for that—my grandmother. I was hesitant to ask, mainly because I'm not a big fan of asking people to do favors for me, especially when it comes to money. Secondly, I recalled the outcome the last time I asked for her help in a major way. However, it was my only option.

I went to my grandmother who was in a care center rehabbing after a recent surgery. I didn't know if the condition and state she was in would work to my advantage or not. After beating around the bush for a few minutes, I told her I needed one thousand dollars and explained what it was for and outlined my expenses on a piece of scrap paper. I made sure to include I would use 10% to pay my tithes. She is big on that. After a few additional questions and the opportunity to rummage the thought through her head for a minute, she approved my request. I don't know if it was the medication or what, but it went smoother than I envisioned. I got the help I needed and prepared myself for a summer which consisted of only sleep, food, and football.

We were deep into the summer, training daily. From weightlifting to running hills to agility drills in the sandbox, we were conditioning our bodies like madmen, getting ready for our upcoming season. We kept two clocks in our weight room. One was a countdown to our first regular season game. The other was a countdown to our last regular season game, which was against That Team Up North. As training camp began and the days on the clocks continued to dwindle down, I couldn't have been more excited. Our team was ranked number one in the country and I was still ranked with the number one defense. Not working that summer was one of the best choices I could've made. I was more comfortable, prepared, and more ready to play than ever.

Game day finally arrived. And guess what? I was the starting cornerback. That's right, little ol' me, the one who wasn't given a chance by anyone my first day on campus; the one who sat quietly in the wings for four years; the one who almost walked away from football altogether, was starting. It was surreal. I had waited a long time and put in a lot of work. I was excited, yet still not satisfied. I started the game but due to our defensive scheme, there were a lot of plays where I was not on the field. Some people would have been content in that situation. Not me.

We won our first game of the season but our real test came in week two when we traveled to Texas to play the Longhorns. They had beaten us the year before and went on to become National Champions. It was payback time. Especially for me, as in the game the year prior I missed a crucial tackle which would have resulted in a safety and potentially changed the outcome of our game. During the week of practice before the game, some player changes took place and I was tasked with playing another position. In addition to cornerback, I was tasked to also play nickelback. The good news was playing nickelback solved my problem of coming out of the game for certain plays and allowed me to remain on the field for virtually every defensive play. The bad news was, outside of a few weeks of practice, it was a relatively new position for me. But as you've read thus far, you know I was up for the challenge.

Low and behold, I played great at the nickelback position during our game against Texas and it turned out to be a coming out party for me. Up until that game, I was nervous I could've lost my starting spot at anytime, but after our win, I felt I solidified myself for the remainder of the season.

Although I was playing well, it wasn't until the fourth game of the season that I started to generate some buzz outside of the team. Still undefeated, we hosted Penn State on a wet and muddy Saturday afternoon. Midway through the fourth quarter, Penn State was only a possession away from tying the score. On one of their late drives, my teammate intercepted a pass and returned it for a touchdown. Needing a score, they came out the very next possession trying feverishly to move the ball. Racing against the clock, every play was a pass. As I aligned in my position, I recognized a formation Penn State was in, in which they had previous success. The quarterback took the snap and dropped back to pass. He looked my direction as he had two receivers running to get open. Going on a hunch, I let the first receiver go by me, as I believed the quarterback was targeting the second receiver. The quarterback threw the ball. My hunch paid off as I stepped in front of the pass and intercepted the ball. It was nothing but green grass and a sea of red from our fans wearing scarlet colored clothing in front of me. I raced down the sideline and, celebrating in the form of a high step, crossed the goal line. It was my first collegiate touchdown. It sealed the game. It was amazing.

My grandmother attended that Penn State game and from what I heard, she was running in the stands as I was running for the touchdown. I could only imagine her yelling, "Run, Tony, run!" For whatever reason, she called me Tony every now and then. That interception sparked the media's attention and many of the fans. Most probably wondered where I had come from. My plan was to make sure from that point forward I would not be forgotten.

A couple of days after the Penn State game, Coach Tressel stopped me in the locker room. "Tone," he said sternly, "someone sent me an email stating that a player looked to be high stepping as they crossed the end zone. That wasn't you, was it?"

"High stepping? No, not me, coach," I said with a smile.

As the season rolled, so did we. Not only were we winning but we were defeating our opponents by three and four touchdowns. I continued to play well at both nickelback and cornerback. My most productive game of the season came in our eighth contest against the Indiana Hoosiers. I was all over the field making tackles left and right. I ended the game with twelve tackles, four tackles for losses including a sack, and a forced fumble. My play throughout the game awarded me co-Big Ten Player of the Week on defense. The season just kept getting better.

Near the end of the regular season, I had just finished a workout when I got a call from a good friend. As soon as I answered the phone, he yelled out "Congratulations, man!"

"For what?"

He informed me that I was selected as a semi-finalist for the Jim Thorpe Award, which is given to the best defensive back in the country. I was shocked. "Yeah, right!" I responded.

I jetted to a nearby computer and pulled up the list. Sure enough, I was one of eleven players listed as a candidate for the award. I was among a great group of guys, honored to even be considered for such an award. I wanted to win it but I was more focused on finishing the season undefeated.

In time, the second clock in our weight room counted down to our final regular season game against our archrival Michigan. It was a game among games. Already considered one of the greatest rivalries of all time, that game in particular was viewed by many as the Game of the Century. We were both undefeated heading into the contest. We were ranked number one in the country with Michigan following right behind us. With only one team being able to come out victorious, both teams were aware of what was at stake. The winner would be crowned Big Ten Champion as well as get an invitation to play in the National Championship game. Playing at home in front of a crowd of over one hundred thousand in the final game of our regular season and what was to be the seniors' last home game, we were not going to lose.

Michigan opened up the game with a touchdown scoring drive. We came right back down the field and tied the score. After a few more scores by us, and another by Michigan, we were up by two touchdowns going into halftime. I thought we would run away with the game in the second half, but Michigan battled their way back and brought the game within three points late in the fourth quarter. After giving the viewers the exciting game they had hoped for and expected, we were able to hold on to the win. The fans mobbed the field. A win against Michigan is always special, and I had been a part of three other victories, but that win was as great as they come.

We were invited as the top ranked team in the country to play in the National Championship game. Considering our regular season ended in mid-November, a week or two prior to many other teams, we had to wait to find out who our opponent was going to be for the title game. Rumors and speculation pointed to the possibility of us playing Michigan again for the title. Some fancied the ideal, believing we were the two best teams in the country. Others didn't care to see the rematch, especially those who were hard pressed about ruining the rivalry and tradition of us playing each other once per year. Nonetheless, Michigan was not invited. Instead, the Florida Gators was named as our opponent for the title game.

The National Championship Game was scheduled to be played the first week of January, which gave us plenty of time to prepare. Some even suggest it was too much time. Normally during this time, which we call bowl practice, we spend a couple weeks practicing the basics and fundamentals. We spend the final few weeks focusing specifically on our opponent. During a practice in one of the earlier weeks, I was participating in a routine drill and fell and landed on my shoulder. Due to the excruciating pain, I instantly knew it was not a routine fall. As I jogged off the field, I couldn't help but wonder if the injury would prevent me from playing in the game. I immediately went to the trainers and they speculated I had fractured my collarbone.

A visit after practice to the doctor's office confirmed that I had indeed fractured my collarbone. The prognosis of recovery was four to six weeks, which served as good and bad news. The bad was, I would be out of practice for some time, but the good, at least in my mind, was I would be healed enough to play in the most important game of my life.

For majority of my life I had been able to stay away from major injuries, such as my shoulder. I battled normal bumps, bruises and sprains and broke two of my fingers when I was a kid trying to hop over a fence. But like most people, I take for granted how our bodies function unconsciously on a daily basis. I was reminded of that with my shoulder injury. I could no longer perform some of the simplest tasks like putting on deodorant or reaching for the remote. You can imagine my thoughts on getting back to tackling a ball carrier. However, I was determined to be ready to play.

I rehabbed my shoulder like crazy. Pulling, stretching and icing, then repeating. After rehab, I would go out and catch the last bits of practice to stay in tune to our game plan. I was eager to get back on the field as soon as I could. I had made great progress over the first couple weeks, but I still had a long way to go. The true test was seeing how I felt once we got to Arizona and closer to game day.

We arrived in Arizona about ten days prior to the game. I still was not cleared to practice as my shoulder was only about sixty percent healthy. I knew in order for me to play I had to get at least a few practices in. I pushed extra hard on every rehab exercise to increase my shoulder strength and range of motion. After about the fourth or fifth day, I persuaded the training staff that my shoulder was healthy enough for me to give it a go. For the first time in weeks I took to the practice field.

Boy, did I need it. The machine cardio I was doing was no comparison to running around on the field. I practiced with caution, leading with my injured shoulder gingerly and only when needed. On one play, I was defending a receiver deep down the field as the ball was thrown to him. We both jumped high in the air to go after the ball. As gravity pulled me back down to the ground, I landed on the one place I shouldn't have—directly on my injured shoulder. Everything around me seemed to come to a stop as I lay on the ground with my eyes closed. The only thing I could hear was me panting. I didn't want to get up from the ground because I was afraid the pain would kick in. Nervously, I sprung to my feet and realized there was no pain at all. In fact, I was perfectly fine. As my coaches and teammates sighed with relief, I knew I was finally ready to go. The fall actually boosted my confidence and proved that my shoulder was healthy enough for me to get back to tackling ball carriers.

Game day finally arrived; it was time to win a National Championship. About fifteen of us red shirt seniors had experienced a win in the 2002 National Championship game, but we all viewed it from the sideline and none of us had an actual hand in the win. It was our turn to go out and earn the ring. The locker room was full of excitement. Guys went through their routine rituals for preparation. Some bobbed their heads while listening to music. Others got stretched and taped. I was busy getting shot up in the shoulder with pain reliever. It was all or nothing. We took the field for our pre-game warm ups. Cameras were flashing, fans were cheering; it was electric. You could see the focus and determination in the eyes of my teammates. After warm ups, we went back to the locker to gather ourselves before kick-off. Last minute coaching details were shared, and then we took to one knee to recite the Lord's Prayer followed by a customary team affirmation. As we ran back to the field for the start of the game, there was no doubt in my mind that we would be triumphant.

We received the ball first to start the game. Florida kicked off, and surprisingly, kicked the ball right to Ted Ginn Jr., the fastest player on our team. Ted started up the field, made a couple of moves to avoid a few defenders and raced down the sideline for our first score. The crowd went wild. Our entire sidelines were running and jumping for joy and high-fiving one another. It felt good to open the game that way, but I didn't want to get overly excited, as I knew we still had a lot of football to play.

Florida answered right back with a score of their own. Our offense couldn't get anything going on their next possession and Florida scored again after getting the ball back. The same cycle repeated itself once more and

Florida went up 21-7. Finally we brought the deficit back to within a touchdown in the second quarter. Throughout the remainder of the second quarter, Florida capitalized on our costly mistakes and added two more field goals and a touchdown to their tally. The score going into halftime was 34-14.

I was disappointed in our play, but optimistic we had enough time to redeem ourselves in the second half. It was obvious Florida did their homework on us as they seemed to be one step ahead of our every move. Their defense was badgering our offensive to the point where we could not throw the ball. Their offense was meticulously moving the ball, challenging our zone defense by dinking the ball for four or five yards each play. Since we now knew their plan of attack, we made some adjustments at halftime and tried to put them to use in the second half.

Florida received the ball in the second half and our defense played tough. We forced them to punt their first few possessions in the second half. Unfortunately, our offense could not generate any momentum. We were stalled from getting any points. The time on the clock continued to tick away and our chances of making a comeback were slimming down. I kept the faith until only a few minutes remained in the fourth quarter. Florida managed to get another score during that span and we had not. As the time expired, we had suffered our first and last loss of the season. Emotions of anger and disappointment poured from our entire team. Prior to the game we were regarded as one of the best teams to come through Ohio State. Afterwards, it felt as if we were just another team that couldn't quite get it done in the end. I guess it just wasn't meant to be.

Chapter Eleven

NFL: Business First then Football

"There is no security on this earth. There is only opportunity."

–Douglas MacArthur

My senior football season officially came to an end. Although it didn't end as I would have hoped, it was a great run from both a team and individual standpoint. We had accomplished a lot and had reasons to hold our head high. I had accomplished a lot. Months prior, I was no where on the radar. Then out of nowhere I became a starter, a contributor, and the recipient for our team's Bo Rein award, which is voted on by the players and given to the most inspirational player on the team. Despite the successes, there was still a lot of work to do on my end. I had to shift my focus from my team to myself, as it was time to get prepared for the next level: the NFL.

Prior to my senior football season, being a player in the NFL was a lofty goal. Becoming a professional athlete seems to be just about every kid's dream at one point or another, just as it was when I was nine years old, but as I got older, it was hard to fathom it becoming a reality. However, I never stopped dreaming. Over the course of my last season, I built the confidence in myself and convinced others I could compete with the best of the best.

Unfortunately, I didn't get an invite to the NFL combine, which is a workout session for college football's elite athletes to showcase their talents to NFL coaches. I was sort of upset, considering I was a semi-finalist for the Thorpe Award, for crying out loud. Not participating provided me an additional few weeks for my shoulder to strengthen. It probably was the best thing for me, but it meant I only had one shot to woo the coaches and recruiters at OSU's workout session, which we call Pro Day. I trained daily, sometimes even twice per day. I dieted like crazy, eating enough chicken, sweet potatoes, and green beans that afterward I didn't want to come in contact with them for a year. I recall having my mother cook me twenty grilled chicken breasts, which lasted me one week. It was a wild regimen, but I was in the best shape of my life.

Pro Day came and I was ready to perform. Hundreds of people were in attendance. Every NFL team was represented by either a coach or a scout. Many were interested in getting a look at the most recent Heisman Trophy winner, which happened to be our quarterback, but until then, they had to watch me and everyone else. It was show time.

Our first three events included bench press, vertical jump and broad jump. On the bench press, I lifted 225 lbs. twelve times. That wasn't bad considering I only prepared two weeks for it due to my shoulder. I jumped 37.5" on my vertical jump and 10'1" on my broad jump. The next several events included the 40-yard dash, short shuttle, long shuttle, and 3-cone drill. After stripping down to my skivvies, I boasted a time of 4.46 seconds in the 40-yard dash. I was noted completing the short shuttle, my favorite drill, in a staggering 3.95 seconds. My long shuttle and 3-cone was reported at 6.51 and 10.9 seconds, respectively.

After a quick break, we finished our workouts with position drills. I was particularly anxious for position drills because I had spent a lot of time studying and practicing the drills I anticipated we would perform. The organizer called up my group of defensive backs to start, but there was a delay. The problem was we didn't have a designated coach to run the drills or a quarterback to throw us balls.

A nearby coach volunteered to run the drills and someone grabbed a quarterback from a local Division III school to throw to us. Simply put, the coach did not run the drills I had anticipated, and instead of the quarterback throwing catchable balls, he was throwing the football as hard as he could to impress the scouts. I was disappointed in the position drills, but overall, I had a pretty good competitive workout. At that point, all I could do was sit back and wait for the NFL draft.

There was roughly a six-week span from my pro day workout until the NFL draft. Trying not to think about the outcome of the draft was tough. My agent and I projected if I were to be drafted, it would be in the later rounds, but there were too many possibilities to analyze. I felt whatever happened would be God's will. The first day of the draft is the most exciting. The top players are selected and essentially worth millions shortly after. Having a feeling I wouldn't be selected on the first day, I didn't watch. In fact, I kept myself busy by helping my girlfriend's parents move. However, I did keep my cell phone nearby just in case. No calls pertaining to the NFL came through.

The second day of the draft began, which is a lot less glorified and I got a call from the Indianapolis Colts. They said I was on their radar and if things worked out they would consider drafting me. It was assuring to know I had some interests out there. Most of the day went by and I still had not received the infamous phone call. As the last couple of rounds got underway, I started to hope that I did not get drafted, thinking I would have more opportunity as a free agent, where if several teams were interested, I could make the choice of which team to join.

The draft concluded and I was not selected. But minutes after the conclusion, my agent received several calls from various teams which were interested in me. Weighing out the options, I decided to go with the Colts, as they showed the most interest and it appeared to be the best fit.

Emotions ran high during and after my decision of becoming a Colt. I reached out to my family and closest friends to spread the news. There was very little time to celebrate, as all the rookies had to report to a training session the very next week. As luck would have it, I was not the only OSU player who had recently become a Colt. The Colts drafted three of my former teammates, so reporting to rookie training was more of a reunion for us.

After a weekend of practices I returned home. At the time, I still had a month left of school. All I had to do was wrap up a couple of senior projects and the mechanical engineering degree was mine. I earned it. After five years of studying, I was more than ready to be done.

Two weeks after our rookie practices, the full team reported for a weekend mini-camp. During one of the drills, I reached out and grabbed a player's jersey and instantly felt a sharp pain in my shoulder. It happened to be the same shoulder I had injured months before. I tried to continue practicing, but as my shoulder began to stiffen, I knew something was wrong. The team trainers took a look at it and declared I needed a CT scan to fully determine the issue. After receiving the scan I was informed that I had fractured my collarbone. That was not good news. I played the scenario out in my head: the fractured collarbone would keep me from practicing, which would keep me from impressing the coaches, which would ultimately lead to the possibility of me being cut and not making the final roster. Not good. Not to mention after the mini-camp I had to return to Columbus and by league rules could not again participate with the team until after graduation. The approach suggested by the training staff was to simply monitor my shoulder's progress.

Prior to the graduation ceremony I gathered with classmates and had a chance to reflect on our time in engineering—the countless hours we spent desperately trying to understand complex formulas, our many poor test scores, our least favorite classes, but most of all, the friends we made through our academic journey. Then, bummed shoulder and all, I threw on my cap and gown for one of the most accomplished days of my life: graduation.

The ceremony began and former President Bill Clinton gave our commencement address. As bad as I wanted to sit and listen to the former President's speech, I couldn't. Our graduation ceremony took place in our football stadium during the second week of June. It was so hot that day I think even the sun was looking for shade. I know I was. Along with a lot of other people, I found some shade near the concessions. When I returned to my seat, a reporter interviewed me about my thoughts on the former President's speech. I winged it like nobody's business, a little ad lib here, a little ad lib there.

After watching thousands receive their diplomas, I finally got to walk across the stage for mine. Afterward, I united with my family for what was a very special moment for all of us. I was officially done with college and full steam ahead into the professional arena as a football player.

* * *

I returned to Indianapolis after graduation to finish our off-season training. My shoulder was not yet healed, so I was unable to practice. According to the doctors, there had been very little progress in the few weeks I had been away. It started to make many people concerned—coaches, family, and me most of all. My optimistic view of making the team began to shift. It's hard enough as a healthy free agent to make a team, let alone a free agent who is injury prone. I started to get a little down on myself.

Football once again took me to a dark place. Many people can easily understand how football can create physical stress on a person, but most are oblivious to the mental stresses caused by football. It's probably because America's favorite sport is generally portrayed as being all fun and games. But just like anything else, there are highs and lows in professional football. And for most, there are probably more lows than highs.

Weeks continued to go by and my shoulder still hadn't healed. I had the strength and range of motion, but scans showed the bone was fractured. I knew any fair amount of pressure could easily complete the break. I also knew my immediate future was dependent on the recovery of my shoulder. I was desperate to get back on the field, but there was nothing I could do to speed up the healing process. It eventually came to a point where it was no longer in my best interest to quickly recover. Due to not practicing, I had missed my opportunity to impress the coaches, but I had been educated by my agent that I was legally not allowed to be cut while I was injured. So I figured one of two things would happen: either the Colts would cut me and I would have to go to arbitration to receive my compensation, or they would place me on injury reserve for the year and pay me my salary. I was hoping for the latter, but had no idea which direction they would choose.

Training camp kicked off in late July 2007. There was still no exact word on my situation, but prior to our first scheduled practice, all injured players and players recently recovered from injuries had to be evaluated and granted clearance by the team doctor. My fate would soon be revealed. As I sat on the table to be examined, the doctor entered. After a couple of quick pulls and pushes he laid out my options and offered his suggestion.

Option One was to have surgery. The fracture in my bone had not yet mended itself and it didn't seem as if it would on its own. I was told the surgery included a four to six month recovery and rehabilitation timeline, which obviously meant I would miss the season and be placed on injured reserve. Option Two, considering my shoulder had decent strength and range of motion, was to practice and see how my shoulder reacted. The thought was if it withstood, then great; if it broke, then I would revert back to Option One.

Option Two was strongly recommended by the doctor. Without hesitation, I informed him that I didn't feel comfortable practicing since I wasn't one hundred percent healthy and I would rather just have the surgery. The doctor again tried to persuade me into suiting up and taking the field. I was steadfast in my decision and viewed his recommendation as an insult. Being an undrafted rookie, I believe the doctor saw me as naïve. Little did he know I had been educated and brought up to speed on how some teams manipulate players to get them to practice just so they can cut them without repercussions.

Not to say that was the intentions of the Colts, but a friend of mine went through a similar situation where things didn't turn out so great for him. The team physicians convinced him to do a few drills on the practice field. What they didn't tell him was they were going to video him working out. Although he didn't feel he had fully recovered from his injury, he was cut the next day. In that instance the player couldn't argue because the team had his performance on camera and the team could simply point out his performance wasn't up to their standards.

My surgery was scheduled. Instead of having it right away, I opted to wait a few weeks so I could attend the practices and meetings during training camp. Even though I wasn't practicing, I still wanted to experience as much of my first NFL preseason as I could. Training camp wrapped after about three weeks and I then headed back to Ohio for surgery, as I wanted the doctor's from Ohio State to perform the procedure. The surgery went well, and afterward I returned to my grandmother's house so she could care for me, just like old times. But just like old times, after a couple weeks I was again eager to have my own space. Just before my surgery, I found a nice apartment in Indianapolis. The great news was due to my surgery, I didn't have to do any of the moving. Members of my family came together and helped me relocate while I just directed where to put things. It was the best move ever.

I settled myself in a nice two-bedroom apartment, which was relatively close to our practice facility, making an easy daily commute. It took me awhile to get acclimated to my new surroundings and it took me even longer to get used to paying my rental fee, as I paid almost double compared to my college apartment. Some of my other rookie teammates, those who were drafted and paid a good amount of money, opted to purchase a condo or a house instead of renting. But considering I wasn't sure of how long I would remain in Indianapolis, my yearly leased apartment was just fine.

Things at this point were going smoothly. My shoulder recovery was on schedule; I was comfortable in my new residence; and I was happily compensated. What else could I want? Well, there was at least one thing I wanted, or better yet, needed. It wasn't anything crazy or outlandish. In fact, what I wanted is what most guys want: a nice automobile. I mentioned I got my first car when I was sixteen. The Hyundai, later coined "The Monster" due to a missing front grill as the result of an accident, lasted me a few years, but I upgraded my second year in college to a newer car and later a motorcycle. I bought myself a Kawasaki Ninja. It was clean, fast, and just like my first car, it had rims. I had chrome rims this time, though. The bike was a nice toy to have and the ladies loved it, but I gave it away closer to my last year in college because I didn't want to injure myself.

To replace my need for speed, I not only wanted a nice automobile, I wanted a *fast* nice automobile. I searched all around for something which caught my eye. After weeks of model and price comparisons, I found the car I wanted. My fondness of Mercedes Benz weighed heavy in my selection as I had my eye on a 02' Mercedes CL 500. I called the dealer, which was near the Chicago area, to let him know I was interested. We discussed all the details and he told me I could pick the car up in a week. Excited, I purchased a one-way plane ticket to Chicago. A few days later I received a call from the car dealership informing me of some devastating news. After business hours, a car drove onto their lot and crashed into my Mercedes. I listened to the story, waiting for a "just kidding" remark. I got none and I was back to square one. Wanting to use my non-refundable one-way plane ticket, I got on my computer in a hurry to try to find another option.

Although I didn't want to rush my car buying experience, I was desperate. Luckily, I found another Mercedes of the same model which also happened to be in Chicago. In fact, it ended up being a better deal than the original as it was a year newer and had some updated features. I called the dealership and displayed my interest. They said they would have the car ready for me in a few days, which meant I could use the plane ticket I had already purchased. Things seemed to be working out.

The day of my first major purchase dawned. I hopped on a quick plane ride from Columbus to Chicago first thing that morning. In an attempt to avoid having to find ground transportation from the airport to the dealership, the salesman arranged for me to be picked up. At least I thought so. Numerous drivers suited in black with name displays paced back and forth in my vicinity but none were for me. I started to grow impatient after about a ninety minute wait in the airport and numerous calls to the dealership. Eventually I was told by the salesman that due to traffic it would be much easier for me to catch the train to a location close to downtown, where I could then be picked up. Not really having another choice, I did as instructed. Boy, was I nervous. There I was in an unfamiliar city riding a train for my first time. Not to mention I had a case full of cash and only one arm to defend myself, as I was still fresh from surgery. After an hour train ride, I made it to my pickup location and was taken to the dealership. That's where the real fun began.

Although I had arrived to the dealership three hours later than my original scheduled time, the vehicle was still not ready for pick up. I was told it was around the corner getting detailed and should be ready within an hour or so. An hour passed, then two. I approached a manager and began voicing my frustration on the poor customer service I was receiving. I demanded he lower the price of the vehicle. My demand was not met as the manager insisted the vehicle was priced at its lowest point and he would get into trouble if he adjusted the price. He did however pull a one hundred dollar bill out of his pocket and suggested I take it to buy lunch. I took him up on his offer. I returned from lunch an hour later but still no car. I was furious but there wasn't anything I could do. I went there with a one-way ticket with plans to leave with a car to drive back to Indianapolis. They had me by my balls and they knew it. Another several hours passed before the car was ready. I sat in the dealership for a total of eight hours. You would've thought I worked there. I was so ready to go, I didn't even test drive the Mercedes. I sat in the passenger seat while the salesman whipped it around the block. After the quick spin, I signed the paperwork and got out of there as fast as I could. I just wanted that day to be over, as I could've have never imagined a worse car buying experience.

Back in Indianapolis, I settled into my daily routine. Being that I was injured, my only true responsibility was rehabbing my shoulder. I didn't even have to be around the facility much. I would go early, spend a half-day and get out. And since I didn't have to partake in the daily practices and meetings, I got the opportunity to step back and look at the team from sort of a bird's-eye view. While I was in college, current and former NFL players would often visit with our team and share their experiences and thoughts about football. Many had the same message, which was, "Enjoy football at the collegiate level while you can." Their reasoning was because football, and any sport for that matter, at the professional level is simply about business. Their words didn't quite register when I was in college, but once I made it to the NFL, I got to see first hand exactly what they meant. Looking at the big picture, I was able to analyze the Colts' team structure of players and personnel and see how much of a business the NFL actually is—and is it ever cut-throat. Different players are signed and released on a weekly basis. People's livelihoods change in the blink of an eye. Hundreds are cut off yearly from the only thing they know. Frankly, if a player doesn't hold a key role on a team, their job is in jeopardy. At the end of the day, like most businesses, it's all about money.

I consider myself a business-savvy type of guy, so it didn't take long for me to grasp the business side of the NFL and figure out how I could utilize what I had to create my own business. See, I always considered football as a means to an end. I never viewed it as being my claim to fame, and as funny as it may sound, I didn't want football to be my ultimate path to success. Of course, I was never offered a $100 million dollar contract. But I have always viewed success from the business world trumping success from the sports world. For example, if I was given the opportunity to make $100 million dollars by playing football or by building a business, I would definitely do it by building a business. Think about it: at some point my value would no longer be worth $100 million. It happens all the time with professional athletes. Eventually my value in relation to the NFL would dwindle to zero, whereas my business would have the opportunity to increase itself.

Business-wise, one of the first things I looked into was real estate. I knew several people who were successful in buying and restoring distressed properties and then selling or renting them. After doing research, I came across a great opportunity to get my feet wet in the business. With almost every business decision, I move forward only if I am comfortable with the worst-case scenario. In that situation I was comfortable with the worst-case scenario and I bought my first property mid-way through my rookie NFL season. It took a couple months to renovate the property and get all the legal work taken care of, but shortly afterward I was in business with tenants in the property and generating a positive cash flow.

My first business venture couldn't have come at a better time. The football season ended, which also meant so did the paychecks. In the NFL, players receive their entire salary during the regular season, which is seventeen weeks long. Do the math and that leaves thirty-five weeks of little to no compensation for most players. For those who fail to properly budget their finances, thirty-five weeks can get rough. I recall several guys talking about their money woes during the off-season stretch. It was good to have a little extra money coming in.

During the off-season, I took advantage of a business program the NFL offered which focused on real estate. It was very informative and covered a wide range of business techniques and practices. Weeks after completing the program, I seized another opportunity and acquired a second property. The turnaround was even quicker than the first and I had secured a tenant within weeks. At the time I figured if all else failed, I'd buy up 15-20 properties and earn a nice passive income. But I still had my heart set on playing professional football.

* * *

It was late spring of 2008 and about time for football to get started. During April through June, although still considered off-season, teams conduct workouts and light practices. I was anxious to get back in the swing of things as my shoulder was completely healed. It took me a few weeks to regain my strength and endurance, but by the end of our six-week workout program, I was in tip-top shape.

We began our light practices, which included a mini-camp, in mid-May. Since the mini-camp the year prior didn't go so well, I was mindful and prayerful during our practices but cautious I was not. I had something to prove and I was determined to prove it. I had several good practices, working at the cornerback position. While I was improved as a player, I didn't improve on our depth chart. We had a lot of guys playing cornerback; so many that my reps came with the fourth string defense. In order for me to get an honest look, I had to beat out a lot of players. My defensive back coach noticed how I was practicing and suggested I switch over to play the safety position, as it would improve my chances of making the team. Being that I was familiar with the position from playing it in college and it provided a better opportunity, I made the switch. Our practices ended mid-June and we had about six weeks off before training camp opened.

We reported to training camp at the end of July. That year we got to play in the Hall of Fame game and there was a great sense of urgency considering we only had eight days of practice before we played. Like every other training camp it was hot and tiresome but we fought through the first week and made our way to Canton, Ohio for our first pre-season game. As it was my first game in the NFL, I was excited as all get out. Canton is only a short drive from Columbus, so many of my family members were there to cheer me on. I was ready to make them proud.

As the start of the game neared, I waited for my slightly-nervous-but-ready-to-play feeling I usually get before each game. The feeling never came. The game began and I noticed the excitement I once had leading up to the game was no longer present. My emotions were all scrambled. I took the field thinking I would regain my enthusiasm, as my on-field persona tends to take on a character of its own. Although I was vociferous and confident on the field, I knew deep down there was something wrong. I recall being on the field looking around the stands and realizing football was no longer the fun game it used to be. My interest and passion for playing football had sunk and didn't appear it would ever return to the level it was before.

After that first pre-season game, my motivation for making the team and continuing on in the NFL changed. The motivation I had my first year was geared toward living out a childhood dream and accomplishing a goal of becoming a professional athlete. Although my first year didn't go exactly as planned, I still accomplished my goal of making it to the NFL, so that motivation was no longer there. As it was never my intention to become the best player ever, or win an MVP award, the only true motivation I had left was financial gain. I believe majority of the players in the NFL only continue to play because of the financial gain—and when I say majority, I mean like 98%. I can almost assure you if you offer any typical NFL player the opportunity to work in a different profession but maintain their football salary, they would take you up on that offer in a heartbeat.

That led me to question at what point would playing football no longer be worth it? To what extent and how long would I put my body and mind through the physical and mental challenges which come with the game? Those were tough questions that I didn't have the answer to at that time. I did, however, vow to myself that I would not be the guy who kept chasing something which was no longer there. I promised I would leave the game before it got the best of me. I am a firm believer that playing professional sports can hurt a person just as much as it can help them. Often times, professional athletes grow accustom to living a high profile lifestyle during their playing careers and then have a hard time parting ways with their lifestyles once their careers are over and forced to do something else.

The Colts cleared up any doubts I had, as they cut me after the third pre-season game. I wasn't pleased to get the words from whom players called the "Grim Reaper," but neither was I distraught. My preparations for that infamous moment allowed me to accept my dismissal from the team in a positive fashion. Mentally, I was in a good place; I had a sense of clarity. The only thing which bothered me was thinking how I would share the news with my family and friends.

I had a brief conversation with my defensive back coach, packed my locker, and headed to my apartment. As I sat on my couch, I thought about my future and what was next. The first thing I needed to do was move from Indianapolis. I figured I would wait around a few weeks to see if another team picked me up, but I refused to be in standstill mode. Like I said before, I realized the NFL was a business. I also realized the NFL was not the only business at which one could be successful.

The year and a half I spent in Indianapolis with the Colts provided a tremendous opportunity for me to grow in many different areas in my life. I experienced things which one could only dream about; I met people I will never forget; and upon leaving I was ready and even more anxious to take on the world.

Chapter Twelve
CUT, CUT, CUT

"Bite off more than you can chew, then chew it."

–Mary Kay Ash

Several weeks went by after my return to Columbus and I hadn't received word of any team interested in signing me. I kept in shape just in case a call came through, but by no means was I sitting around waiting. Instead, I was full steam ahead with the entrepreneurial mindset of building and maintaining my own businesses.

I had developed two new concepts to add to my portfolio. One was a non-profit organization. I decided early on that I was going to give back, or better yet, pay forward, to the people in and around my community. My second concept was that of a traditional for-profit business in the transportation market. I have to admit, due to the economy, it wasn't the best time to pursue starting a new business, but I am the type of person who, once I get rolling on something, I go out and try to get it done.

Over the years I have come across tons of people who have ideas and aspirations to own their own business. Yet I know of very few who actually try to make it happen. Do you know why that is? It is because they are afraid to fail. See, failure doesn't intimidate me. If I am comfortable with the worst-case scenario, then I move forward.

Just as I was getting deep into my planning, I got a call from the Detroit Lions in early November in which they offered to sign me to their practice squad. Although I didn't want to take a break from what I had going on, I figured I would join the club and make some quick money. And quick it was. I got to Detroit and had three practices with the team before they left for an away game. Since I was on practice squad, I didn't travel. The day after the team returned, I received a call in which I was informed I was being released. It was one of the quickest weeks of my life. Of course getting cut for the second time was just as unpleasant as the first, but it wasn't all bad. I made about five grand for my three days of work, got health insurance for an entire year, and scored a pair of tickets for a Madonna concert. Not to mention that was the 2009 Lions team which ended up going a whole season without winning a game.

I wasted no time once I got back home. I pitched my business concept to my good friend and former teammate Roy Hall, who decided to partner with me on the venture. Within months our business, which was a luxury transportation service, was up and running. Keep in mind I still was renting out my properties, so at the time I was running two businesses plus the non-profit. I was flat out trying to make it happen, living by the quote from Abraham Lincoln: "Good things come to those who wait, but only the things left over by those who hustle."

* * *

I grew to understand when the weather broke and the buds and flowers began to blossom, it was time for me to get into football mode. It was spring of 2009 and for the first time in years I wasn't thinking football. I was busy trying to make sure my businesses generated revenue. The decisions I made with the money I received from my first year in the NFL eliminated the pressure of me having to get a traditional nine-to-five job right away. At some point I wanted to put my engineering degree to use and gain experience in that area, but for the time being, I was just fine being my own boss.

As my mind was so far away from football, I was shaken one spring afternoon when I received a call from the Detroit Lions. Considering they had cut me after only a week of practice months before, it was ironic they called me. They offered me an opportunity to rejoin their team as they were in their off-season training. I was so thrown off that I couldn't even give them an answer right away. I told them I needed to talk to my agent and would call them back. Really, I just needed time to diagnose the situation and figure out what was the best move for me. I wasn't naïve and I knew they only wanted me as an extra body for their minicamp. However, there was a part of me which felt I should give it one last shot. As they had an abysmal season the year prior, there was a huge overhaul in coaches and personnel and the thought of a fresh start was appealing. I wrestled with the decision for thirty minutes or so but ultimately chose to rejoin the team and give it one more go.

My time in Detroit lasted longer than I anticipated, which turned out to have both positive and negative drawbacks. Although I had another opportunity to play in the NFL, the biggest challenge I faced dealt with finances. My income started to decrease and my expenses were increasing. Neither my business partner nor I was in Columbus at the time and it was tough operating our new transportation business from afar. As we decided to go against the grain and start the business in the early stages of a recession, without one of us being the face of the company and pushing it in our local market, the revenue it generated was not even remotely close to the expenses of the business. So not only was the business becoming unprofitable, eventually my partner and I had to reach into our own pockets to cover costs. The bottom line was the longer I stayed in Detroit, the less chance I had of having a successful business.

To make matters worse, I was also having financial issues with my properties. They say when it rains, it pours, and was it ever pouring. My tenants weren't paying their rent. During the first year I didn't have any issues with rental payments, but as that second year rolled around, those same tenants stopped paying. Knowing the economy was worsening and people were being laid off, I tried to be as lenient as I could, but at the end of the day I had bills to pay, too. It came down to the bills getting paid from my personal money.

Regardless of how much a person makes, if their expenses are more than their income, there is a problem. It means nothing for an individual to earn a $1 million salary if there expenses are $1.1 million. I had to figure out a way to reverse my financial situation by increasing my income and decreasing my expenses. The quickest way I knew to increase my income was to finish the off-season with the Lions and make it through their final cuts for the regular season. If I took that route, there was virtually no way to sustain our transportation business. It ended up not being that hard of a decision as the logical method to decrease expenses was to cease operations. In the summer of 2009 my partner and I decided to cut our losses from the business and move on. One of the greatest things I believe a person can learn in business, and in life, is when to move on. Often times, the same wave which can take you high can also take you under.

2009 was a terrible year for me financially. Many people questioned the closing of our transportation business. Yes, the business itself failed, but I didn't walk away empty handed. One of the greatest positives of failing is you are able to eliminate that failure as a possibility for success and move on to the next. I realized the transportation business was not for me at that time. Did it mean I would be fearful to start another business in the future? Absolutely not. I learned a great deal from my mistakes with the transportation business and vowed to be better in certain areas with my next venture. As far as the properties, the lesson learned there was to try to acquire tenants who paid their rent, which is easier said than done. I eventually did get new tenants and the financial issues melted away.

* * *

I made it through the Lions off-season training and practices and was looking forward to entering training camp. They had me playing the safety position, which was the same position I ended with the Colts. Just as every other phase of my life, I knew earning a spot on the team was going to be a hard fought battle, especially due to the fact the Lions drafted a safety that year in the second round.

The day before training camp began, as I was making sure everything was in order before I took off, I got a call from the infamous Lions once again. First off, I never understood why the Lions always called me directly without first talking to my agent. They were the only team which ever did that. The call this time was not to sign me but to cut me. In order to sign the rookie safety they had drafted, they had to make room and release a player under contract. That player happened to be me. As always, I was disappointed but I understood the business, hence why when I was told I still needed to come to Detroit to do an exit physical, which is part of the process of being released, I demanded they book me a flight. The front office personnel were livid because they assumed I was going to drive as I would have if I was attending training camp. But there was no way in the world I was going to drive three hours just so they could sign a few papers and then drive another three hours back home. They ended up booking me a flight from Columbus to Detroit, which is less than an hour in the air, but hey, that's business for you.

A few days after Detroit cut me, I got picked up by the San Diego Chargers. Going all the way out West to play was a different feel for me, but I just went with the flow. San Diego was beautiful and the weather was amazing, but it was too far for me. For four weeks I hardly spoke to any of my family and friends due to the time difference. When I got out of practice it was too late to call and the absolute worst was when people tried to call me. They always called first thing in the morning Ohio time, which were the wee hours of the morning California time. I competed hard and gave my all, but once again I was released during the final cuts.

Playing for three different teams in less than three years was a sign that it was time to explore a different profession permanently. I thought it was a good time to put my degree to use and look at opportunities in the field of engineering. The problem was I didn't know where to start. The couple of jobs I had in college were not exactly in line with my degree and due to football I never got a true chance to intern or co-op. Considering the many different career paths one can choose with a mechanical engineering degree, I needed to figure out which direction I wanted to pursue.

I started by narrowing my focus to three distinct career paths. First was the automotive industry. As a kid, I always had a fascination with cars. Since I didn't have a father or a male presence in my life growing up, I never really got under the hood so to speak but fancied them from afar. I especially fancied Lamborghinis. I drew a picture of one in the second grade and told myself that one day I would have one. The closest I've gotten thus far was a test drive a few years back but I'm keeping hope alive. At times I've imagined myself designing and test driving cars of the future so it was an area I considered exploring as a career.

A second path, stemming from a childhood love of playing cops and robbers, was to pursue a career dealing with weapons and gadgets. Since I was the only child in the household, many times I would be the cop and the robber. I guess that's a Gemini for you. After seeing the movie In Too Deep, I wanted to be an undercover cop. The irony lies in the fact that although I wanted to be an undercover cop, I never wanted to go through the regimen of being a uniformed cop. I just wanted to dive straight in. I thought it would be cool to have a job where you shoot and blow stuff up on a daily basis. Before the NFL, I could've headed in that direction. Approaching college graduation, I interviewed with an organization called Battelle in which one of their departments designs and develops weaponry for clients such as the U.S. Military. It happened to be my only true job interview coming out of college. The interview went well but the NFL seemed more enticing at the time.

The last career path I considered was the building and construction industry. One reason was because of my dealings with property and real estate. Another influence came from the time I spent working at an architecture firm for a few weeks in college. The ways in which buildings are designed and built intrigue me. So much so that at one point in time I even considered going back to school to obtain a degree in architecture. I figured with a degree in architecture and engineering, one day I could design my entire house inside and out. After meeting with several advisors in the architectural field and analyzing the unfavorable timing of becoming an architect due to the economy, I decided that was not in my best interest.

Once I had identified the career paths in which I had interest, it was time to dig deeper into those specific areas and see if I could find a job. I did everything I could think of. I searched the web, looked in classifieds, applied for positions, made phone calls—everything. For several weeks it was all to no avail. I did gain interest from one engineering firm which led to a non-formal meeting with one of the principals of the company, but they didn't have a position for me at the time.

* * *

As I continued to ramp up my search for job opportunities, I received a call one Monday evening from my agent informing me that the Cincinnati Bengals wanted me to come workout for them. When a team calls, they usually want you to come right away. They were expecting me to be in Cincinnati that night so I could work out first thing in the morning. The call put me in limbo. For starters, my mind had gotten away from football and I was concentrating on finding a job and building my other businesses. In fact, the night I received the call, I had a big business meeting at my house for a network marketing company I had just got involved with, not to mention it was the week of Thanksgiving and dinner was to be hosted at my house that year. I was stuck.

Once again I faced laying down my plans and responsibilities for an opportunity to play football. I couldn't help but think of the outcome which took place in Detroit. Lord knows I didn't want a repeat. I went back and forth with my agent discussing the pros and cons. I came to the conclusion that I would go and workout, but there were only certain drills I was willing to do. I had not been consistently training for football, so I was not prepared to run a 40-yard dash or some of the other miscellaneous drills teams have you do. I had been fortunate in the past as I never had to really workout for a team; they would usually just sign me. I told my agent if they asked me to run a 40, I was going to get in my car and return home. And I was dead serious about that.

The business meeting at my house wrapped up around nine o'clock that Monday evening. It took another hour or so to clean up and then I had to get myself ready to drive an hour and a half down to Cincinnati. By this time, I regretted my decision to go. I left the house just before midnight and arrived at a hotel in downtown Cincinnati close to 1:30 a.m. I was exhausted. I made my way up to my room and as I entered and turned on the lights, I found someone already asleep in the room. My first thought was that I had been directed to the wrong room—how rude. Startled, the guy woke up and I found out that we were both there for tryouts. I put my bags on the floor while chuckling at the fact I had awakened this guy from a cold sleep. We spoke briefly and discovered we were both trying out for the same position. Go figure. We then hit the sheets as we were expected to be up and ready in only a few hours.

It felt like I had just closed my eyes when morning dawned. Our first order of business was to get checked out by the team doctor at a nearby hospital. Following that two-hour ordeal, we made our way to the football stadium to conduct our workouts. The facility was fairly empty as it was a Tuesday and Tuesday's are off days for players in the

NFL. Our escort showed us the way to the locker room to get dressed. It was a little weird as it wasn't the team locker room we were directed to but a small locker room which the referees use. We got dressed quickly but no one came back to get us for quite some time. We had a chance to converse and share stories as we waited.

Eventually, a gentleman came in and revealed some not so good news to both of us. The other guy that I was working out with received the worst of it. He was told the Bengals were no longer interested in working him out and that someone would take him to the airport. The news for me was not as bad; the plan for me to workout had not changed, just the timing of my workout. I was told that I had a few more hours to wait.

Obviously, the news didn't upset me as much as it did the other guy, but I was still irritated. I was in a small locker room with no one around and I hadn't eaten anything all day. I get really upset when I don't eat. A few minutes later, one of the team trainers walked in and greeted me. That made my day. It turned out I knew him, as he happened to work for the Colts when I played for them. I told him what was going on and he offered to take me back to the hotel so I could get something to eat and pass the time.

I made my way back to the hotel and grabbed the first seat in the restaurant. I began to feel a little bit better about myself and my irritation faded once my food arrived. But then I received a call while I was eating from the Bengals staff saying they were ready to work me out. I couldn't believe it. They told me that I had a few hours and it hadn't even been thirty minutes. I told them that I was eating and due to their miscommunication, they would have to give me at least an hour to get back to the stadium. They agreed.

Back at the stadium, it was finally time for my workout. Being that it was my first true tryout for a team post college, I was a little nervous. I became even more nervous when I saw the head coach and a few assistant coaches watching my drills. The nerves settled and I gave it my all just as I would in any other setting. Immediately following my workouts, I was told I would be signed to the practice team. Once again, just like that, my life was flipped in an instant.

Every team I played for, with the exception of San Diego, provided me the luxury of being close to home. Cincinnati was the closest. Being only a short car ride away from Columbus was beneficial as it allowed me to travel back and forth. After signing on Tuesday, I practiced both Wednesday and Thursday and then headed to Columbus Thursday evening to be with my family, as it was Thanksgiving. I got up early on Friday morning and returned back to Cincinnati for practice. We had a home game my first week, so I stayed around and returned to Columbus after our Monday practice.

I remember driving in from Cincinnati that Monday and being within minutes from my house in Columbus when I received a call from a 513 area code. It was Monday, the day when most NFL players get cut, and I didn't have a good feeling about the call, so I let it go to my voicemail. I listened to the message as soon as it came through and sure enough it was a Bengals staff member on the other end telling me I was going to be released. Another one-weeker for me just like Detroit. To be professional, I returned the call and desperately hoped I didn't have to drive all the way back to Cincinnati to sign my release papers. I was so relieved when I was told I didn't have to. That brings us to cut number five, if you're keeping count.

Getting cut by the Bengals after only one week provided me with an opportunity I wouldn't have had otherwise. The network marketing company I had gotten involved with prior to joining the Bengals was holding a huge conference out in California which I had initially planned on attending. I had to cancel my plans once I signed with the Bengals, but as soon as I got cut the plans were back on. I got cut by Cincinnati on Monday and was out in California by Friday. The conference turned out to be a huge success with over 20,000 attendees and provided a great sense of encouragement and motivation for my new and old businesses. I was excited to get back to Columbus and apply what I had learned, but my efforts were stalled once more. I returned to Columbus on Monday, and low and behold, on Tuesday the Bengals called me back to rejoin the team. I felt like I was being tinkered with, getting signed one week, cut the next and then signed again. I went back anyway.

I finished the season with the Bengals, and fortunately didn't get cut. Our 2009 team had a pretty good run as we won our division and made it to the playoffs, but we lost our first playoff game against the New York Jets. After the season ended, I signed another contract with the Bengals to return for the 2010 season. Believing in my heart it was my last go-round, I figured I would ride out.

As soon as season ended, I shifted my focus back to my businesses. I no longer concentrated on finding a job because there was no way I could commit to any company with football being in the picture. My properties were still holding steady, so I devoted most of my attention to my latest venture of the network marketing business. With network marketing, it's all about momentum. It took me a couple of weeks to get going, but once I got the hang of it, my business started building. Now there are many different network-marketing businesses out there, but I felt comfortable with the products and services we provided. We didn't offer a juice or a lotion, but services people already had or used in their homes, such as cable television, home security and phone lines. I went hard for a couple of months trying to build and maintain that momentum.

Before I knew it, it was time to get back to football and off-season training. Although I had signed a contract with the Bengals, I seriously considered not returning to the team. I found out that the Bengals, unlike other teams I played for, did not pay for living accommodations for players during the off-season. That forced me to reanalyze my financial situation. I could not afford to go through five months of off-season training and get paid peanuts while paying for an apartment or hotel in Cincinnati and then get cut. I was to the point where I needed to earn a consistent, substantial amount of money to cover my expenses. The money I made my first year in the NFL along with my investments had pretty much carried me up until that point, but I knew I couldn't survive much longer without a steady income.

I didn't want to walk away from what I considered my last opportunity to play ball, so I devised a plan in which I could minimize my expenses while being in Cincinnati. The plan involved limiting my overnight stays in Cincinnati and commuting for training as often as I could. The cost of gas was lower than the cost of a hotel, so the more I could commute, the more money I could save. It was my only option to stay with the team. Luckily, I had a teammate from Columbus who enjoyed commuting, so we took turns driving. My routine lasted about six weeks and ended with me being cut in early May 2010 for my sixth and final time. I made up my mind there was no coming back for me. In order to truly move forward in my life, I needed that chapter to come to a close.

Football had been a part of my life for close to fifteen years. I have learned so many life lessons and have taken so much away from the sport. Playing in the National Football League provided me with an experience which very few can claim and gave me a platform to get a glimpse of what the world truly has to offer. For that, the sport and my experiences will always be something I cherish, but it was time for me to move on and reach greater heights.

Sidebar Speaking of which, are you happy with your job, career or financial situation? If the answer is no, then do something about it. I know that's easier said than done, but if you don't make a move to better your situation, who will?

Too often I talk with people who are unhappy with their jobs, stuck in a career which they do not enjoy, or are just plain tired of living paycheck to paycheck. I truly believe those who wholeheartedly desire to do and obtain something better in life will have the opportunity at some point. The question is, will you seize that opportunity when it arises?

Not everyone has the desire to be great. I use the term "great" in the sense of living life to the fullest and trying to reach as far as you can. Some people are content being average, while others are just fine being below average. Everyone has an opinion of what average entails, but I perceive being average as someone having the known ability to do more than what they are currently doing. Notice I didn't put a quantitative measure against being great or average because that can't be judged by how much money you make or how many degrees you hold. A person who makes five million dollars a year can be average, especially if they know they can make ten million. The same holds true for someone who has a Ph.D. or is skilled in a specific area, yet fails to effectively utilize that knowledge or skill set.

I know the majority of the people reading this do not have a five million dollar salary or hold a Ph.D. (including myself). I'm just trying to shoot it straight. I'm not claiming to share something you've never heard before. Sometimes it just resonates better over time or from a different source.

As I said, I come in contact with people from all walks of life who are unhappy with their jobs or financial situations. Most of the time these people have ideas on how they can better their situation and themselves. For some, it is as simple as getting a higher paying job. For others it might be a career switch to something they are passionate about, while quite a few people actually want to stop working for someone else and take the road of entrepreneurship. As I talk with these people, I hear the excitement in their voices about their ideas and goals and I wonder why they haven't made a move to pursue their passion. If you listen long enough and ask the right questions, the person will tell you exactly why they haven't pursued it. As I am not big on excuses, I tend to look past the typical complaints about not having enough time or having too much responsibility. More often than not, it all boils down to—you guessed it—that people are afraid to fail.

It's understandable how a husband with three kids may have reservations about leaving his secure job to pursue his childhood dream of becoming an actor. At the same time, that husband who wants to be great but views his life as average will have a hard time finding true happiness. As husbands and wives become mothers and fathers, a sense of responsibility sets in and parents no longer look to please themselves first, often times pushing their dreams aside, sometimes indefinitely. I am all for the "do what you got to do" mentality, but what greater example can a parent show to their kids than mom or dad, despite all obstacles, was able to reach a longed-for accomplishment?

Or what about the mother who for years has worked tirelessly for others to make ends meet for her children and is now ready to take her talents to the next level by starting her own business? With little business experience and only a concept, it's easy to see where the uneasiness may lie.

Yet every successful company was once just a concept. That is the first step—and it is an important step. Although many people have great concepts, most people default in taking their concept to the next step, which is putting it down on paper. Why is that? A common explanation is the person over-analyzes his or her idea and shoots it down before it even develops, which usually stems from having a fear of failure. Or better yet, the person shares their ideas with someone else prematurely and is met with remarks such as, "That's stupid," or "That will never work." The thought of failure reveals itself as a common denominator.

These are just a couple of examples which many people struggle with. Are you in a similar scenario? When was the last time you thought about changing your situation? Have you acted on it yet? Life is too short to let the fear of failure get in the way of you being great. In fact, instead of fearing failure, this is the perfect time to be waiting to fail. I know that may sound kind of weird, but take notice I said waiting to fail, not wanting to fail. If you want to fail, then this is clearly not the book you should be reading. On the other hand, waiting to fail puts you in a frame of mind to do two things: first, it allows you not to have to deal with failure because it hasn't come yet, hence the keyword waiting; secondly, it allows you to prepare for failure in case it does occur.

Failing is not all bad. In many situations, a dose of failure can be advantageous and actually help you in the long run. Remember my luxury transportation company? Roy and I thought we had a great idea on our hands and were certain people in our inner circle would help explode our business by using our service. We were so confident that we never sat down and laid out a true marketing plan before we started the business. It wasn't until three or four months later when we realized we needed to utilize a different approach to gain business.

The bottom line is, not having a legit marketing plan before we started the business was a huge mistake and was ultimately one of the reasons the business didn't last long. But was it all bad that our business failed? No. Don't get me wrong, I could have used the several thousands of dollars I lost in the deal, but I walked away from that business with an invaluable experience. Ever since I received my expensive marketing lesson, one of my main focuses of every business or project I get involved with is analyzing and understanding how the product or service is going to be marketed. Because of that focus, I have been more productive and successful with all my projects.

For those of you who are beginning to feel energized and confident enough to start making some changes to your situation, here's a bit of advice. As a disclaimer, by no means am I suggesting that you go to work tomorrow and put in your resignation. I am suggesting you think hard about what you want out of life and make an effort to make it happen. I also suggest that you do due diligence and make sure what you would like to accomplish can be done in a positive manner with a positive outcome.

As a rule of thumb, I always look at the worst-case scenario of any major decision I am facing. If I am absolutely comfortable with the worst-case scenario, then and only then do I grant myself permission to move forward. The key is once you do decide to move forward, put your head down and go full steam ahead. The worst thing you can do is second guess yourself or be timid in your approach. People who sit on the fence tend to miss opportunities on both sides of the field.

Finally, don't let a failed attempt stop you from moving forward. Sometimes we muster up enough courage to take one step, but when we get hit and have to take a step back we want to give up. It's no secret that some of the world's brightest people and greatest inventions were discovered after hundreds of attempts. If you do fail, that's fine, as that possibility is simply eliminated from the pool of potential successes and you are able to move on to the next possibility.

Due to my entrepreneurial spirit, I am constantly searching for new businesses and ideas in which I can be successful. I have tried many. From traditional businesses to networking marketing businesses to internet businesses, I have dabbled in them all, many with no success. But instead of letting my shortcomings put a halt to my business progression, I embrace those shortcomings with the faith that I am one step closer to discovering the venture which will bless me with more than I can imagine.

If you get nothing else out of this sidebar, don't be afraid to fail. Don't be afraid to do. Don't be afraid to dream. Just because you're not a kid anymore doesn't mean you can't dream. Remember that mansion you dreamed about living in when you were younger? Or how about that fancy sports car you dreamed you would own one day? What happened to those dreams? I can guarantee that you never dreamed about living in a Cracker Jack box of a house in a neighborhood of look-alike homes while driving a Kia Spectra (apologies to Kia Spectra owners). All I am trying to say is don't let the fear of failure keep you from reaching what God has planned and purposed for you and what you have purposed for yourself. Strive to be great.

Remember, it's not the things people do that they regret the most, but the things they don't do.

Chapter Thirteen
WAITING TO FAIL

"The greatest discovery is that a human being can alter his life by altering his attitude of mind."

–William James

With football over for good, I could finally focus on what I needed to do to put myself in the best possible position to win. I was having some success with the network marketing business, but it wasn't enough. I decided to pull back from that venture and totally submerse my efforts into finding a job and building my non-profit organization. Roy Hall and I had similar programs in the Ohio area, so once again we joined forces and established the DRIVEN Foundation.

Giving back, in my opinion, is an important concept. Having all the success in the world means very little if you don't use your platform and or resources to help others. Because of my upbringing, I understand the needs young children and families face due to poverty. The DRIVEN Foundation allows us to address and support some of those needs. Since inception, the foundation has grown, serving the needs of youth and underprivileged families throughout Central Ohio with an array of programs ranging from fitness to literacy to food outreach.

I also got back to searching for engineering job opportunities with the eagerness of being able to fully commit if something came along. Similar to the year prior, I went awhile before I got any type of response from any company. I was on the brink of ending my search when I finally got a reply from a local engineering firm, Dynamix Engineering. I was invited in for an interview which went well and was then invited back for a second. After the second interview, I thought I had the job in the bag. I was just waiting for the "You're hired" response. A week went by, then two, then three. I sent an email to follow up to see if the company had made any decisions yet.

Another three weeks went by. Feeling desperate and losing hope, I sent a second follow up email. I vowed it would be my last. Several days went by and still no response. Then I ran across the president of the company at a local event. The funny thing is, we greeted each other and I shook his hand, but I couldn't remember where I recognized him from. It wasn't until after we went our separate ways that I realized who he was. Seeing him at that event did something because he contacted me a few days later and asked me to lunch. We went to lunch and I was presented with a job offer that day. I took the offer, put my mechanical engineering degree to use, and I am still with the firm today, aiding in the design and construction of buildings across the Midwest.

* * *

Unlike Orie's dad's prophecy, "You ain't gonna be nothin', boy!" I didn't amount to nothing. On the contrary, I amounted to several *somethings*: NFL player, businessman, engineer, and motivational speaker. No amount of discouragement and doubt from anyone ever kept me down—and you shouldn't let it keep you down, either. 'You shouldn't let circumstances dictate your direction except to point you in the right direction: up.

So, what's next for me, you ask? Who knows: maybe another book, business venture, or cool engineering design which earns LEED Platinum status. I am letting God lead the way and show me what He wants me to do. I have come to the conclusion that people act on things in life based off of two principles: fear or faith. I act in faith, unafraid to fail. By taking action, I postpone failure. When failure occurs, I view it as a stepping stone to future success down other avenues. So you see, waiting to fail isn't such a bad thing. Whether I'm working for the DRIVEN Foundation, Dynamix, or simply at life, you'll find me hard at work, waiting to fail.

Waiting to Fail

Bonus Sidebar

I figured since I will be a newlywed in 2012, I will leave you with a bonus sidebar for the road!

The relationship I believes carries the greatest fear of failure is the intimate relationship between two people, such as a marriage or longtime girlfriend/boyfriend. This fear of failure can come from a couple sources. The first source consists of one or both partners being so fearful of a failed or bad relationship that they don't truly commit themselves to the relationship. An example of this is a woman who has been hurt in the past and never wants to experience that feeling again. Sometimes the fear originates in a man who doesn't know how to treat a woman well and he is afraid to admit it. It is almost a fact that this sort of fear will cause a split. At some point you have to let go of the fear or it will be the demise of the relationship.

The second source is a fear of cutting ties and being alone. Love often gets in the way and keeps us holding on for as long as we can, but when that love fades and the main ingredient keeping the relationship alive is convenience or fear, then, "Houston, we have a problem." I'm not talking about a couple which has had an argument or two; I'm talking about a person who knows that the relationship they're in is unhealthy. Whether it is from physical, verbal, mental or sexual abuse, undue stress, selfishness, or incompatibility, an unhealthy relationship needs to be addressed and either resolved or dissolved.

Women are perhaps the most prone to this problem. While they have more opportunities to work and have careers and make a life for themselves without a husband or children, many still look to a man for financial support as well as emotional fulfillment. Some women stay with abusive boyfriends and spouses because they think they won't find anyone better, or their current man doesn't hit them as much as the last one. Fear of being alone overrides logic and causes them to stay in dangerous relationships.

Fear of being single and therefore seen as a failure to commit to or thrive in a relationship also keeps people in unhealthy situations. While the old school routine of going to college, getting married, and starting a family is no longer the norm, our society still links success with marriage. A man or woman may have a great career but someone will inevitably ask, "When are you going to settle down and get married?" So despite their financial and business success, the lack of a wedding ring, home in the suburbs, and 2.5 kids means they've failed in some way.

People who fear a failed relationship often care more about how others are going to feel than themselves. They'll ask questions like, "What will my family think?" or "What will my friends say?" They fear the potential shame of people thinking of them as failures. They also may fear starting over intimately, financially, and socially. They have a hard time envisioning their life without their partner as positive, so they opt to remain in the relationship and situation.

There are factors other than fear which have bearing on the status of a relationship, one of the biggest being children. No loving parent wants to miss time with his or her child. Co-parenting and joint custody is never fair on at least one parent and deprives children of the optimum amount of time spent with that parent.

Money is probably the next biggest factor. Have you ever heard the saying, "It's cheaper to keep her"? A divorce or breakup can wreck havoc on finances. I'm not just talking about the transition from living off two incomes to one, but splitting property and possessions, accommodating child support or alimony . . . the list goes on.

Please don't think that I am encouraging break-ups or divorces. The divorce rate is high enough already. But the bottom line is that sometimes relationships just don't work out. Just as one shouldn't have the fear to commit to a relationship, and one sure shouldn't have the fear to relinquish a relationship. In either case, don't be afraid to fail.

ABOUT THE AUTHOR

Antonio Smith is a former collegiate and professional football player, and current mechanical engineer. He is a community leader and helped establish the DRIVEN Foundation, an Ohio non-profit organization geared toward helping youth and underprivileged families.

His journey has provided him with the necessary tools to capture and motivate the minds of people from all ages. Antonio resides in Ohio, and enjoys spending his free time with family and friends.

You can visit him at
www.speakerantoniosmith.com